Enjoying Hummingbirds

In the Wild & In Your Yard

Larry and Terrie Gates

STACKPOLE
BOOKS

0 11557 03421 9

Published by
STACKPOLE BOOKS
5067 Ritter Road
Mechanicsburg, PA 17055
www.stackpolebooks.com

Gates, Larry, 1942–
    Enjoying hummingbirds : in the wild and in your yard / by Larry and Terrie Gates. —1st ed.
        p. cm.
    ISBN-13: 978-0-8117-3421-9
    ISBN-10: 0-8117-3421-8
    1. Hummingbirds. I. Gates, Terrie, 1945– II. Title.

QL696.A558G38 2007
598.7'64—dc22

Printed in Canada

10 9 8 7 6 5 4 3 2 1

First Edition

Cover design by Caroline Stover

Special thanks to those who provided photos for the book:
Terrie Gates
Damon Calderwood
Tony Godfrey
Bill Schmoker
Aspects, Inc
Alamy

Contents

INTRODUCTION

KNOWING HUMMINGBIRDS

ENJOYING HUMMINGBIRDS

HUMMINGBIRDS AND CULTURE

APPENDIXES

For our dear friend, Sally Spofford,
who loved all things wild.

INTRODUCTION

THE JOY OF HUMMINGBIRDS

Who can resist watching a hummingbird as it hovers in front of a red flower, plunges deep inside, then paddles back out with yellow pollen on its face and bill? Hummingbirds are the tiniest birds in the world. They seem to defy the law of gravity as they fly up, down, backwards, sideways, and even upside down. When sunlight catches their iridescent feathers, they glitter like cut gems.

HOW THIS BOOK IS ORGANIZED

This book is divided into three parts. The first section answers these questions: What is a hummingbird? What hummingbirds can be seen in the United States and Canada? How does one identify them? The second section answers another question: What activities can a person engage in if he or she wants to pursue an interest in hummingbirds? The third section answers this final question: What role have hummingbirds played in the collective imagination of people, past and present, who live in the Americas?

In the first section we describe how hummingbirds fit into the overall community of birds, and we discuss, in some detail, the behavior of hummingbirds—their daily routines, their mating and nest building, the care they give their young, and the fights they have with one another. We describe their endless search for food, the special relationship they have with plants, their migration, and their continued survival as individuals and as a species. We describe the anatomy of hummingbirds and explain how they fly. Attention is given to hazards hummingbirds encounter from predators, severe weather, parasites, disease, habitat destruction, and pesticides. Did you know, for example, that praying mantises have been known to snatch hummingbirds out of the air?

The first section also details what species of hummingbird occur in the United States and Canada. It describes which ones to expect in the region where you live and gives you specific information about how to tell different species apart.

In the second section of the book, attention is given to methods of feeding hummingbirds and attracting hummingbirds to your yard. We make suggestions for selecting feeders, making nectar, and setting up a hummingbird garden. We provide information that will help you select the best plants to buy for a garden in the region where you live.

Next we suggest a wide variety of ways that you can pursue hummingbirds as a hobby, avocation, or even vocation. This includes backyard activities, organizations to join, meetings to attend, Web sites to visit, photography, bird banding, amateur ornithology, care of injured birds, and more. We then make suggestions for planning a hummingbird vacation, either in the United States or south of the border, where many more species can be seen.

In the final section of the book, we discuss how hummingbirds have been depicted in myths, legends, history, popular culture, and literature.

Throughout this book we share fun and interesting experiences we have had in the hummingbird-rich mountains of southeastern Arizona. We also incorporate hummingbird experiences passed on to us by visitors at the Hummingbird Web Site (www.hummingbirdworld.com), which we have maintained since 1997.

We must warn you that the love of hummingbirds, like the love of mountains or oceans, can be highly contagious. It may even be incurable!

THE WORLD OF HUMMINGBIRDS

In many respects, the whole western hemisphere is the land of the hummingbird. These glittering, fairylike creatures are unknown in other parts of the world, but they occur in all parts of the United States except for Hawaii and the northern regions of Alaska. They can be seen across southern Canada and along Canada's west coast. In Mexico, as well as in Central and South America, the number of species dazzles the imagination. In Ecuador alone, there are more than 160 types of hummingbirds. In the world, there are about 329 species. The most recently described is the Gorgeted Puffleg, which was discovered in a cloud forest in Colombia in 2005 and confirmed in 2007.

The best-known and most popular hummingbird is the Ruby-throated. This tiny, green-backed bird is a national icon, appearing endlessly in decorative art, poetry, and folklore. The signature feature of the male is its gleaming red throat. No other bird has captured the imagination of the people in the eastern United States and southern Canada quite like this one. No hummingbird in the world is better known. As the only species that nests east of central Texas or the Great Plains, the Ruby-throat is the joy of flower gardeners, nature lovers, and people who just enjoy sitting out in their backyards. One Ruby-throated Hummingbird is all it takes to turn a nice day into a perfect day. In late summer or in fall when migration is at its peak, Ruby-throats can become abundant. There are records of hundreds, even thousands, occurring at a single migration hot spot on a single day.

In the West there are several other species, but no Ruby-throats. The feisty, copper-colored Rufous Hummingbird is abundant in migration in the states that border the Pacific Ocean as well as in the Rocky Mountains and in the deserts of the southwest. The Anna's Hummingbird brings happiness even to apartment dwellers all along the West Coast. They are also commonly seen in gardens in places like Phoenix or Tucson. Allen's Hummingbirds are common in many parts of California. The tiny Calliope Hummingbird and the Broad-tailed Hummingbird are regularly seen in summer throughout the Rocky Mountains. We have sat at a restaurant in the mountains of New Mexico, watching dozens of Broad-tailed and Calliope Hummingbirds feeding and fighting just a few feet away from us on the other side of a picture window. The Costa's Hummingbird is a popular garden bird in southwestern deserts. Sometimes they nest on wind chimes. With very few exceptions, Americans can enjoy hummingbirds right where they live.

OUR VERY OWN BACKYARD HUMMINGBIRDS

We live in a beautiful place. Every morning we wake to the towering pink cliffs at the mouth of Cave Creek Canyon. Beyond the cliffs we see the evergreen high country of the Chiricahua

Mountains. Looking the other way, we see Chihuahuan desert. Our house, near a creek that meanders out from a dark green valley just above us, is a perfect place to enjoy hummingbirds. Our proximity to the Sierra Madre Mountains of Mexico makes possible a variety of hummingbird species far greater than that seen in any

Blue-throated Hummingbird

other region of the United States. We have had twelve different hummingbird species in our yard and we have seen three other species within a mile of our house.

Two species of hummingbird appear at our feeders just about every day of the year: the Magnificent and the Blue-throated. We have seen them feeding while snow is falling and we have seen them sipping our sugar-water on outrageously hot days in late June. These two species are considerably larger than the other North American hummingbirds. We are especially fortunate in having the Blue-throated year-round. Our small village, Portal, Arizona, is the most reliable location in the United States to see this remarkable bird. The Blue-throats fight frequently, especially with each other. We have seen them tangle in midair like jousting medieval knights.

Black-chinned Hummingbird

Our hummingbird garden

Calliope Hummingbird

Our other perennial visitor—the dark, handsome Magnificent Hummingbird—also looks like a fierce warrior, but it's actually a big sissy. We've seen it chased away by hummingbirds half its size.

Our most common hummingbird in the breeding season is the Black-chinned. During the breeding season we also see Broad-billed and Violet-crowned Hummingbirds. In spring, late summer, and fall, we see Broad-tailed Hummingbirds, Rufous Hummingbirds, Calliope Hummingbirds, and Anna's Hummingbirds. The Broad-tailed is superficially quite similar to the Ruby-throated Hummingbird of the east. It is subtly different both in the green coloration of the back and in the red of the throat; also, it has a much bigger tail. The wings of the male Broad-tailed make a whirring sound when it flies. We can tell by sound if one is in the feeding area.

The male Rufous Hummingbird is an iridescent copper color; though small, he is a tougher and more persistent fighter than even the Blue-throat. The Calliope Hummingbird is the smallest bird in North America. Its throat is boldly striped with red and white, like an old-fashioned barber pole or a candy cane. The male Anna's is red on the helmet, as well as on the gorget.

Costa's Hummingbird

Costa's Hummingbirds and Allen's Hummingbirds often show up in mid-summer. The male Costa's has a purple helmet and a matching purple gorget that flares out on both sides. In the field, the Allen's Hummingbirds are usually impossible to distinguish from the very similar Rufous Hummingbirds. (Bird banders and researchers can tell them apart when they catch them in traps, take measurements, and closely examine their tail feathers.)

Within walking distance of our house we have seen White-eared Hummingbirds, Berylline Hummingbirds, and a Plain-capped Starthroat. We consider ourselves blessed to live in our own private hummingbird heaven.

There are places across the United States where far more individual hummingbirds can be seen in a single day. We have more variety; other places have more individuals. Actually, you can have splendid experiences with very few hummingbirds. A single hummingbird seen once a year—or once in a lifetime—is a joy worth savoring. So look around. Plant flowers with abundant nectar. Put up a sugar-water feeder. Your chances of seeing hummingbirds in your backyard or very close to home are probably better than you imagine. You may find fewer species than us—indeed, you may find just one—but if your life is enriched and you have a good time watching, what else really matters? The Ruby-throated Hummingbird was our favorite bird and the only species of hummingbird we had ever seen before we made our first trip to Arizona. Our experience solely with Ruby-throateds was totally satisfying for more than twenty years. We still love to go back east and see them.

Probably the most amazing hummingbird phenomenon of recent decades has been the mysterious and wonderful appearance of several western hummingbird species in the Southeast. It now happens regularly in winter, especially in places like New Orleans and Baton Rouge, Louisiana. Winter hummingbirds from the West are also occurring all along the Gulf Coast as well as in Florida. To a lesser extent, winter hummingbirds from the west have been seen along the East Coast, and occasional winter records are now occurring in places like the Midwest or southeastern Canada. Rufous is the most common vagrant, but, as we will describe later, several other species have occurred.

HUMMINGBIRDS AS A SOURCE OF ENDLESS WONDER

The pleasures of hummingbird watching, like the pleasures of any other hobby, can be greatly enhanced as we learn interesting facts. Here are a few:

- Hummingbirds are the smallest birds on earth and also the smallest of all the warm-blooded vertebrates. Without feathers, hummingbirds are about the size of a bumblebee. It is worth noting, though, that—compared to other birds— hummingbirds have bigger brains in proportion to total body size.
- Hummingbirds often eat more than half their total weight in a single day, and they have been known to consume twice their body weight in water in one 24-hour period. This gives new meaning to the phrase, "Eat like a bird."

- Hummingbirds have the fastest wing beats of all the birds. This is about 80 beats per second in direct flight and up to 200 beats per second in the power dives some of the males do during courtship.
- Many Rufous Hummingbirds annually migrate back and forth from Alaska to Mexico; this is more than 5,400 miles round-trip!

In the pages that follow we attempt to tell you everything you ever wanted to know about hummingbirds.

Knowing Hummingbirds

CHAPTER ONE

WHAT IS A HUMMINGBIRD?

How Hummingbirds are Like and Unlike Other Birds

Though they fly much like insects, hummingbirds are indeed birds. Like other avian species, they are warm-blooded. Their bodies are covered with feathers, their forelimbs have been modified into wings, and they have hollow bones. Hummingbirds do, however, differ in numerous ways from almost all other birds. Because of this they have their own special family, which is called Trochilidae.

Swifts and hummingbirds fly in a similar manner, and both can assume a torpid state at night. They both have weak legs, which make them unable to walk. Both hummingbirds and swifts lay white elliptical-shaped eggs. There are significant differences, however, and the jury is still out with regard to how closely these two groups of birds should be categorized. The recent Sibley-Ahlquist system of taxonomy does not lump hummingbirds and swifts together; it places hummingbirds in a separate order.

It is widely assumed that hummingbirds originated in South America, where there is a remarkably large number of hummingbird species, including a subgroup called hermits that lack the iridescent sparkle that characterizes other hummingbirds.

Compared to other birds, hummingbirds have a small clutch size, usually only two eggs. Though rare exceptions have been reported, hummingbirds do not bond with a mate, and hummingbird males do not tend to nests as males of most other avian species do.

Hummingbirds also have a closer relationship to flowers than most other birds. Many plants have flowers structured and arrayed in ways that are conducive to hummingbird activity. Penstemons, for example, are spaced just far enough apart to accommodate the beating wings of hummingbirds, and their tube-shaped, nectar-filled flowers are perfect for a hummingbird bill. While feasting on the sweetness inside bright-colored blossoms, hummingbirds unknowingly assist in pollination. It's a win-win situation: The flowers diversify their gene pool, and the hummingbirds get food. As we watch the behavior of hummingbirds, we get a lesson about the interdependence of all living things.

Though hummingbirds are found only in the Americas, there are unrelated birds in other parts of the world—sunbirds, for example—that also take nectar from flowers. There is recent, surprising evidence that birds similar to hummingbirds once occurred in Europe. In 2004 Dr. Gerald Mayr reported finding two 30-million-year-old fossils, with remarkable resemblance to modern-day hummingbirds, at a clay pit in Germany.

The Anatomy of a Hummingbird

Hummingbirds are the smallest birds in the world. It would be impossible for any bird to be smaller than a hummingbird, because—as a warm-blooded animal—the bird couldn't eat fast and often enough to keep up with its body's needs. The smallest hummingbird of all is the Bee Hummingbird of Cuba, which weighs only 1.8 grams. The most common hummingbirds in the United States—the Rufous, the Ruby-throated, and the Black-chinned—all weigh about three grams.

Hummingbirds live their life in the fast lane. They have a remarkably rapid metabolism, which is 20 times faster than that of a barnyard chicken. Hummingbirds breathe rapidly—about 250 inhalations per minute. They also have the most rapid heartbeat of any bird. It has been estimated that the cranberry-size heart of a Blue-throated Hummingbird is capable of thumping 1,260 times per minute. When a hummingbird is perched on a branch, the heart typically beats about 500 times a minute.

Hummingbirds are able to fly like a helicopter—hovering, flying swiftly or slowly, and quickly changing directions. They can do this partly because of the unusually large and powerful muscles that lift their wings. Another reason for the remarkably agile flight of hummingbirds is that about 70 percent of their wing is supported by handlike bones with joints that are fused for extra strength. The upper wing bone can rotate more than 180 degrees in the shoulder

PARTS OF A HUMMINGBIRD

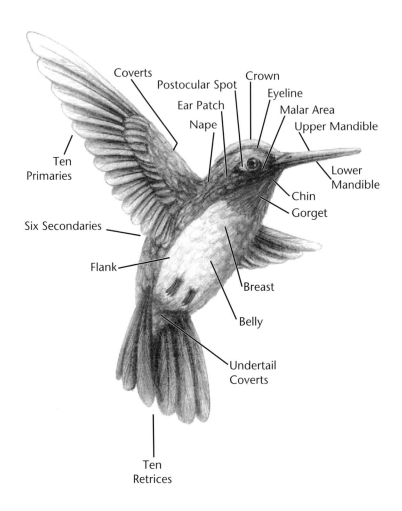

Coverts

Postocular Spot

Ear Patch

Nape

Crown

Eyeline

Malar Area

Upper Mandible

Lower Mandible

Ten Primaries

Chin

Gorget

Six Secondaries

Flank

Breast

Belly

Undertail Coverts

Ten Retrices

socket. For their size, hummingbirds also have a huge, deeply keeled breastbone.

A distinctive characteristic of hummingbirds is their long, needle-like bill, which—to many people's surprise—opens like the bill of any other bird. This becomes apparent when a hummingbird feeds babies at a nest. In some species the bill is slightly decurved. Though the bill is black or gray in most species, there are a couple of U.S. species that have a mostly red bill. The obvious purpose of the bill is to probe deep into flowers in search of nectar.

Lucifer Hummingbird

There are more than 1,000 feathers on a hummingbird, most of which are quite small and tightly packed. The feathers on the wings and tail are larger and less snugly crowded together. The tail has ten feathers. In some species the tail feathers are arrayed in a round formation; in others the tail is forked, wedge-shaped, or relatively straight on the end. More unusual tail shapes can occur in Central and South American species. Each wing of a hummingbird has sixteen flight feathers—six on the inner wing and ten on the outer wing. The outer feathers are called primaries and the inner ones are called secondaries. The leading edges of the wings are lined above and below with tiny feathers called coverts. The feathered linings on the shoulders are called scapulars.

Rufous Hummingbird tail

The most remarkable thing about hummingbird feathers is that, especially on the throat, they can be quite iridescent. Iridescence typically occurs only in the outer third of a hummingbird's feather, but—since the feathers overlap—these tiny birds can show large masses of glittering color. The iridescence of the feathers is primarily caused by light passing through a substance with a higher refractive index than air. A similar phenomenon can be observed on soap bubbles. The iridescent portion of a hummingbird feather is packed with tiny mosaiclike platelets, which occur in stacked layers to make a film of varying thickness. The color red is reflected by thick films, while the color violet is reflected by thin films. Color is also affected by microscopic air bubbles within the platelets. Hummingbirds have pigment in their feathers just as other birds do. The colors of a hummingbird's feathers can appear to change as the bird is seen from different angles. The throat of a male

Rufous Hummingbird wing

hummingbird—called the gorget—can appear to be red from certain angles, green or blue from different angles, and black from yet other angles.

THE GORGET

Most male hummingbirds have a brilliantly colored and iridescent throat patch that contrasts with the rest of the bird's plumage. This is called the gorget. Gorgets can be red, purple, blue, lime green, black, or other colors. In certain circumstances male hummingbirds orient themselves so that the sun will cause the gorget to glitter.

Female Magnificent Hummingbird

Hummingbird Metabolism

When flying, hummingbirds have a higher rate of metabolism that any of Earth's creatures, except for certain insects. In order to sustain the rapid beating of their wings, hummingbirds can sometimes have a heart rate of more than 1,000 beats per second. The only way to maintain this high metabolism is to eat frequently. Hummingbirds are active from dawn until dusk, and they make hundreds of visits to flowers every day. They are never more than a few hours from starvation. They do rest, but not for long periods of time.

So how do they make it through the night when they do no feeding at all? Research has shown that hummingbirds can slow down their metabolism during the dark hours.

Hummingbird Behavior

Flight

A hummingbird's wing is flexible at the shoulder but inflexible at the wrist. While other birds get their flight power from the downstroke only, hummingbirds have strength on the upstroke as well. In the powerful upstroke, hummingbirds can change the angle of the wing so that several different types of thrusts can occur on the downstroke. Hummingbirds flap their wings from 15 to 100 times a second. The rapidly beating wings make a humming sound, which gives these birds their name. Differing pitches of the wing stroke interact with rotary movements in the outer portion of the wing to allow the hummingbird to fly right, left, up, down, backwards, and even upside down.

Doug Altshuler, a researcher at the University of California at Riverside, has discovered that the electric impulses driving a hummingbird's wing are more similar to that of insects than other birds. This explains why the flapping motions of hummingbird

Broad-billed Hummingbird in flight

wings produce more power per unit of mass than that of any other vertebrate.

When hovering, hummingbirds hold their bodies upright and flap their wings horizontally in a shallow figure eight. As the wings swing back they tilt flat for a moment before the wings are drawn. Slight tilts of the wings act in much the same way that helicopter blades do, allowing slow and precise travel from blossom to blossom, then in and out of blossoms. When hummingbirds want to hang in the air at one precise point, they do it with no apparent effort. But their rapidly beating wings appear as a blur. Most hummingbirds normally flap their wings about 50 or so times a second. This means all we can see is a vague smudge at the birds' shoulders. The Blue-throated and Magnificent Hummingbirds can be exceptions to this rule. Sometimes they flap their wings slowly enough for individual wing beats to be perceived—though not while hovering. While other bird species flex their wings at the wrist, hummingbirds use their wings more like oars.

Hummingbirds can hover and move about with even more precision than a helicopter. Scientists have been amazed by their ability, even when it is windy, to maintain a stable position in space and then dip in and out of flower blossoms with pinpoint accuracy. Researchers at the University of Alberta have recently determined that a specific nucleus in the brain of a hummingbird is considerably larger, relative to brain size, than the same area in other birds. It is believed that this specialization makes it possible for hummingbirds to fly with such precision while beating their wings at mind-boggling speeds.

The tiny feet of hummingbirds are almost useless except for perching. If a hummer wants to travel two inches, it must fly. Hummingbirds lift from perches without pushing off; they rise entirely on their own power, flapping their wings at almost full speed before lifting. Though they fly very fast, hummingbirds can suddenly stop and make a soft landing. They are so light they do not build up much momentum.

Numerous researchers have studied hummingbird flight from the perspective of aerodynamics. In one of the best studies, a biophysicist named Douglas Warrick studied Rufous

Hummingbirds in a wind tunnel. He and his colleagues found that these tiny birds produced 75 percent of their weight support during the downstroke and 25 percent of their weight support on the upstroke. They concluded that hummingbirds hang in the air in a way that is different, though in some ways similar, to the flight of insects. Other studies of hummingbird flight have been done using high-speed video.

Feeding

Because of their fast breathing rate, fast heartbeat, and relatively high body temperature, hummingbirds need to feed every ten minutes or so. They may consume two-thirds of their body weight in a single day. A major part of a hummingbirds' diet is sugar from flower nectar and tree sap. Hummingbirds also need protein in order to build muscles, so they eat small insects and pollen.

As a hummingbird approaches brightly colored flowers one can sometimes see a long translucent tongue spilling out of its beak, licking the air. The front half of a hummingbird's tongue is split in two and frayed along the outside edge. The troughlike tongue has grooves on its sides, which are useful for catching insects whether they are in the air, on leaves, or entangled in spiderwebs. Though the tongue is about the same length as the bird's bill, it can be pushed forward with elongated bones at its root to probe deep into tubular flowers. A hummingbird can flick its tongue about 13 times a second. Contrary to popular opinion, hummingbirds do not suck nectar but lap it up with their tongue.

Hummers have good memories that enable them to remember food sources from previous years. As they feed, hummers accidentally collect pollen. When they move from flower to flower, they spread the pollen and help the flowers to reproduce. Many flowers, like penstemons, seem to be specifically designed to accommodate hummingbirds.

Territory

Male and female hummingbirds establish separate territories—she to build a nest and feed her young—he just to protect a reliable food source. The male takes no interest in nests or the care and feeding of babies. When females enter his territory, he does aerial displays to keep them away.

Displays and Courtship

Hummingbirds communicate with one another by making visual displays. Males sometimes raise the feathers bordering the gorget and toss their heads from side to side while uttering shrill sounds. Females and young are more likely to do perched displays in which they spread their tail feathers to show the white tips.

Sometimes both males and females do shuttle flights, which are rapid back-and-forth movements in front of another bird. During the shuttle flight, the tail and gorget may be displayed.

Dive displays are only done by the males. At key points in the dive, buzzing, whistling, or popping sounds might be made with the wing feathers or the vocal cords. The trajectory of the dive is U-shaped. At the top of the arc, the bird may be quite high in the air.

The narrowly focused shuttle dance of the male is usually part of a courtship ritual. After finding a willing female, he flies in front of her in short, rapid arcs. The dance field may be about ten inches wide.

We once saw a Black-chinned Hummingbird shuttle like this in front of a female that was perched in a mesquite. Looking intimidated, she moved her head back and forth, watching his awesome aerial movements, which were only inches from her face; then she hung upside down by her toes as he mounted her. Since little is known about hummingbird copulation, we have no idea as to whether or not this was unusual behavior.

When watching the flight and dive displays of the hummingbird males, it is often difficult to tell whether one is witnessing aggression or an invitation to copulation. If the display is directed at another male, at a hummingbird of a different species, or at a creature that is not a hummingbird at all, it is obviously aggression. If the dive is directed toward a female of the same species, it could be aggression or wooing, or possibly both at the same time.

In the breeding season, the male Anna's Hummingbird engages in courtship displays when he encounters a female in his territory. Often the female starts building a nest and goes looking for a male to mate with before the nest is finished. Typically she may enter his territory and begin feeding on flowers. He may immediately chase her or he may watch her until she perches, then show a dive display that often appears to be more aggressive than romantic. After the dive, a chase will begin. She, like a pursued wood nymph, will lead the male to either her nesting territory or some place that is neutral. Then she will find a perch and face him. At this point the male may emit a high-intensity song or engage in a shuttle display. This consists of an aerial swaying back and forth in front of a perched female, who turns her head to directly face his every move—as if intimidated. All the while the male's bill points down and he sings buzz notes. She may then allow him to copulate with her, or she may fly away again.

The males may swoop up and down in a U-shaped or J-shaped pattern, or they may rapidly fly back and forth in what would be the arc of a huge pendulum. They position themselves in the air so that the sun will reflect the iridescence of their boldly colored throats toward the object of their attention. In their ecstatic flight, they may fly high in the sky, repeatedly swoop down to within inches of the female, then climb high for another dive. They often make strange noises during this flight.

The spectacular display of the Anna's Hummingbird starts with the male singing one or two sets of raspy notes while he hovers several feet over his audience, which may be anything from a female of its species to a human being. While wavering, he ascends to a height of 60 to 130 feet and then plummets straight down, ending

his dive with a loud noise. At the bottom of his dive he curls back up in a circular arc with his bill pointed down. All during this display, he orients himself so that his red gorget and helmet reflect a maximum amount of brilliant color either to attract a female or to intimidate an intruder.

Similar but usually less elaborate courtship rituals take place in other hummingbird species. The courtship flight of a male Allen's Hummingbird, for example, begins with a rapid pendulumlike arc of about 25 feet, then concludes with a rapid dive from about 100 feet up in the air.

In some hummingbird species (mostly those south of the border), the males gather in communities, which are called leks. Then they all sing together to try to entice females to come into the neighborhood, pick out partners, and engage in the brief encounters that will make them pregnant.

Fighting

Hummingbirds compete for nectar and insects. They guard their territories fiercely, perching high near flowering bushes or feeders. Anna's Hummingbird puffs itself up to look large. In duels, the hummers sometimes stab with their bills and use their claws as weapons. They may fan out their tails and they may erect their feathers. Fighting hummingbirds sometimes collide with a loud thud. We recently saw two hummingbirds fighting over a feeder. The bird that was perched raised its head and held out its wings while the other dive-bombed it from above. The fight became more and more vicious as bills locked and both birds dropped to the ground. One bird ended up on top of the other. After ten seconds of stillness, the weaker of the two was released and flew away across a dry creek bed, yielding, at least for the moment, the feeder they both refused to share.

Sometimes a dueling hummingbird will hang upside down from a branch. This was once thought to be a posture of submission, but close observation shows it to be a stance that can show both strength and dominance.

Actually, hummers are seldom harmed by these fights, though they may occasionally lose a few back feathers. Their instincts tell them not to risk damage to their precious bills. Also, they fight less when food is scarce. Occasionally hummers attack other birds, even hawks and crows. Though they don't attack human beings, it's sometimes slightly frightening to have a whirring blur of feathers and a needle-like beak zoom by just a few inches from your face.

Blue-throated Hummingbird in an aggressive display

Song

Hummers make a variety of unmusical calls—from deep guttural sounds to high-pitched chirps. A few, like the Anna's and Blue-throat, mutter a feeble, scratchy, sputtering song, which is used by the male to establish and protect a territory. Many hummers will emit a loud chatter when their territory is invaded.

Grooming

Hummers preen themselves with their bills and claws. Using oil from a gland near their tail, they groom their wings, abdomen, tail feathers, and back. Stroke by stroke they tend to the veins of each feather. Hummers often groom their heads and necks with their feet, using the front three claws like a comb. When they scratch their heads and necks they typically hold their feathers erect and lift a leg over a wing. Sometimes they will groom their beaks or necks by rubbing them against a twig. Often a grooming hummer will grasp its bill and slide along it with its claws. While grooming, they may stretch both wings up over their back. They frequently fluff themselves up and shake.

Costa's Hummingbird preening

Feather maintenance is essential

Hummers also take sunbaths, positioning the breast toward the sun and fluffing out their feathers. They extend their necks and spread their tails. They may stretch one wing then the other, and then lower their heads while stretching the wings upward.

> ## CARRYING A PURSE
> Occasionally a hummingbird that seems to be carrying a purse will be seen. The purse can be almost as large as the hummingbird. Close inspection will reveal that the "purse" is actually a clump from a spiderweb, accidentally snagged while the hummingbird was snatching trapped insects.

Bathing

Hummingbirds like to take baths on wet leaves or in shallow puddles. They flutter their wings or pull them straight back while lifting their widely spread tails and dipping their chins and bellies into the water. Sometimes a bathing hummer will throw its head back to toss droplets on its back. Hummingbirds sometimes sit in the rain on a bare branch with feathers ruffled up. Also, they like to dart in and out of the fine mist put out by lawn sprinklers. A friend told us she was watering her flowers with a garden hose when a hummingbird flew several times through the mist she was creating. Eventually the bird got soaked and landed on her hand. After bathing, hummingbirds preen, pulling individual feathers through their beak.

Broad-billed Hummingbird bathing on a leaf

Sleep

Hummingbirds sleep with the neck retracted and head forward, the bill pointed up at a sharp angle, and the feathers fluffed. On cold nights some hummingbirds go into torpor, slowing down their metabolism and mimicking death so they can cling to fragile life until the warm sun returns. The torpor is similar to hibernation but briefer.

Hummingbird Nests

In general, male hummingbirds do not contribute in any way to the building of nests or the care of young; this responsibility falls to the females. There are a just a few reports of male Ruby-throated and Rufous Hummingbirds incubating eggs, and there is at least one report of a male Anna's Hummingbird feeding young. These are exceptions and not the rule.

The typical hummingbird nest is a tiny woven cup, about the size of half an English walnut shell. The outer part is covered with moss and plant fibers. Sometimes it is shingled with lichens. The rest is made of plant down and spiderwebs. Most often the nest is built on a tree branch. Hummingbirds do not reuse the same nest, but often build again at the same location, occasionally right on top of the old nest.

Rufous Hummingbird nest

A hummingbird's nest usually has two white eggs. They are less than half an inch long. The incubation period is typically from two to a little more than three weeks. It is a remarkable sight when the mother hummingbird comes with food and two little heads pop up. The mother perches on the side of the nest, arches her back, stretches her neck, lifts her head, and holds her bill down to regurgitate nectar and half-digested insects to her babies. Her throat swells and she pumps her beak like a sewing needle.

An adult Rufous Hummingbird approaches the nest

Feeding hungry nestlings

Baby Rufous Hummingbirds exercise their wings

Hummingbird Migration

Most of the hummingbirds in the United States and Canada go south for the winter. Some linger in warmer regions of the United States, especially along the Pacific Coast, in regions close to the Mexican border, and on the Gulf Coast from Texas to Florida. One of the great mysteries of nature is how a creature so small as a hummingbird could travel hundreds or even thousands of miles and end up in the correct place. Hummingbirds typically take the same routes and have the same stopover places. The northward spring route may, in some cases, be different from the southward route taken in late summer or fall. There is evidence that hummingbirds reappear in the same gardens year after year. Undoubtedly these tiny birds are genetically programmed to migrate, and in their wee brains there must be some map of where to go. The mechanisms through which they navigate are poorly understood. They could possibly use the position of the stars, visual landmarks, shorelines, magnetic fields, or even subsonic sounds from oceans that are hundreds of miles away.

Hummingbirds in migration do not fly as high as many other birds do. Often they fly just over the treetops. When flying over open water, hummingbirds tend to fly just over the tops of the waves. There is speculation that Ruby-throated Hummingbirds may sometimes fly under the curl of a wave, using the swelling water as a windbreak.

MIGRATING ON THE BACKS OF GEESE

Many people think that migrating hummingbirds are hitchhikers that ride on the backs of geese. This is not true. Hummingbirds and geese do not even migrate at the same time of the year.

Migration requires a considerable amount of energy. Hummingbirds will fatten up before a long journey, gaining a significant amount of weight. It is not unusual for them to double their weight just before migrating. In flight they will burn up most of this fat. When hummingbirds first arrive on their breeding grounds, they feed voraciously from flowers and insects. Many newly arrived hummingbirds have also been seen licking up sap from holes drilled in trees by certain woodpeckers, which are called sapsuckers.

Hummingbirds encounter many hazards while in migration. Some may cross large deserts, and others may cross large bodies of water. On stopovers they may encounter predators that are not on their breeding grounds. They can fly into windows, tall buildings, and radio towers. Storms can be a major hazard, while exhaustion and muscle depletion are yet other dangers. We once met someone who had seen a dead hummingbird fall out of a clear blue sky.

As a general rule, the males migrate before the females, and birds that nest farther north migrate later in spring and earlier in fall than birds that migrate to southern states.

The trigger for migration are hormonal changes which, in turn, are triggered by the slowly changing number of hours and minutes of daylight in a 24-hour period. Unlike other birds, hummingbirds do not migrate in flocks. Nevertheless, many hummingbirds can end up at the same stopover place at the same time if it is a good feeding ground.

Hummingbirds migrate in the daytime with only one known exception: Some Ruby-throats are forced to fly all night when engaging in a long journey across the Gulf of Mexico.

It has been estimated that it takes Ruby-throated Hummingbirds in New England about two weeks to get from their breeding grounds to their wintering grounds.

Predators and Other Dangerous Encounters

We live in a world where the big creatures eat the little creatures. And hummingbirds are in the small category. Among the more common predators are other birds. Small hawks, like kestrels or Sharp-shinned Hawks, can be a menace to hummingbirds—as can crows, jays, orioles, and certain flycatchers. Terrie once gasped in horror as she saw a Brown-crested Flycatcher swoop down, catch a Violet-crowned Hummingbird, and then land on a branch with the hummer hanging out of both sides of its mouth. Some of her birding friends said that's impossible: a Violet-crowned is too big and a Brown-crested Flycatcher is too small. But she saw it! Here's an even stranger story: At the Desert Museum in Tucson, a Black-chinned Hummingbird was seen investigating the face of a captive mountain lion. The lion opened its mouth, extended its neck, grabbed the hummingbird in its teeth, and swallowed it whole.

Roadrunners are especially adept at catching hummingbirds. We had one that learned to stand near a nectar feeder—as still as a wood carving—then suddenly thrust out its neck like a striking rattlesnake to knock a hummingbird to the ground or snatch it right out of the air. That roadrunner could swallow a hummingbird in a single gulp. We saw another roadrunner that patiently stalked hummingbirds by standing on a roof, poking its head over the edge to snatch hummingbirds that were feeding from a feeder that was hanging from the eave.

There are also records of hummingbirds being caught and eaten by snakes, lizards, and frogs. In South America there is a giant spider that often catches hummingbirds. Smaller spiders have been known to eat hummingbirds after they become entangled in a web, while gathering material to build a nest. Though extremely rare, there have been a couple of reports of hummingbirds being caught by dragonflies. One of our friends saw a praying mantis catch and eat a Rufous Hummingbird.

The most vulnerable time for a hummingbird is before it becomes an adult. Snakes and jays can eat the eggs or the nestlings. Also, young, inept, and inexperienced birds are easy to catch.

In spite of all these potential predators, hummingbirds are more likely to die from other causes—disease, starvation, dehydration, parasites, and cold weather—than from predators. Lice, mites, and ticks can take a toll on the hummingbird population. Hummers also can get tapeworms, flukes, and roundworms. They have been known to perish from being impaled on a thorn or a prickly leaf. Some expire while attempting to cross the Gulf of Mexico in bad weather, and a hummingbird's heart can simply give out during a long migration.

Finally, we must not forget that human activities and structures can be a major hazard to hummingbirds. Hummingbirds sometimes fly into glass windows. They can be hit by a car. They can accidentally jam their bill into a window screen. They can fly into attics or garages and not be able to find a way out. Hummingbirds can also die because of pesticides, pollution, and habitat loss.

> **TIP**
>
> By placing a decal of a hawk silhouette or a spiderweb on a window near your feeders, you could possibly save a hummingbird's life.

CHAPTER TWO

THE HUMMINGBIRDS OF NORTH AMERICA

The 16 hummingbirds we describe in this chapter all occur annually in the United States. A few have breeding ranges that extend just slightly north of the Mexican border, and two are rare and localized, though they do nest in the United States every year.

Allen's Hummingbird

Selasphorus sasin

SIZE Small (3.2–3.5 inches)

HABITAT The breeding range of the Allen's Hummingbird is along the Pacific Coast where there are summer fogs.

OVERALL IMPRESSION A bronze-gold and green hummingbird.

CLAIM TO FAME Limited range, early migration, early departure.

RANGE The main population of this species breeds from Ventura County in southern California to Coos County in the southeastern corner of Oregon. Although most Allen's Hummingbirds spend the winter in Mexico, a nonmigratory subspecies is found in the Channel Islands as well as the nearby Palos Verdes Peninsula of southern California. In mid- to late-summer migration, these birds occur in southern Arizona where they are almost impossible to tell apart from the more abundant Rufous Hummingbirds, which pass through at the same time.

DESCRIPTION Allen's Hummingbirds have straight, medium-length bills. The adult male is orange-brown with a copper-red throat and a green back. The adult female is bronze-green above, and her underparts are white. She is cinnamon colored on her flanks, sides, and the edges of the rump, and has dark flecks on her throat. Immature Allen's Hummingbirds have variable plumage but resemble the adult female. Immature males may have a partial gorget.

IDENTIFICATION TIPS In most circumstances it is impossible to distinguish Allen's Hummingbirds from Rufous Hummingbirds. If the bird breeds in California or southwestern Oregon, it is an Allen's. If a rufous-colored male has a full gorget and an all-green back, it is most likely (but not certainly) an Allen's.

BEHAVIOR Allen's Hummingbirds arrive in California in midwinter. After establishing territories in coastal scrub, males defend their domain with spectacular diving displays. They can often be seen perching on leafless, horizontal branches where they enjoy a good view of their estate. The females usually nest in more densely vegetated areas where there are trees.

The male Allen's Hummingbird is highly aggressive. He will chase away any other hummingbird that enters his territory. He sometimes vanquishes birds much larger than himself.

The male Allen's Hummingbird often engages in a dive display aimed either at a female Allen's Hummingbird or at some other bird perceived to be an intruder.

In this display the male etches the letter U in the air, rising about 25 feet on either side. After doing this several times, the bird spirals up 75 or more feet, then dives down. Male Allen's also do short back-and-forth shuttle displays to impress intruders or potential mates.

Male Allen's Hummingbirds begin leaving their territories and migrating south as early as mid-May, often before females have finished caring for their young.

NESTS Some female Allen's Hummingbirds build nests that straddle tree branches as high as 50 feet above the ground. Other nests are constructed in low vines or on fern fronds, sometimes as low as a few inches off the ground. Two white eggs are laid and then incubated for about seventeen to twentytwo days. Fledglings leave the nest about twentytwo to twentyfive days later. As is true of almost all other hummingbird species, the males take no role in the building of the nest or the care of the young.

GENERAL COMMENTS Since the migrating Allen's and Rufous hummingbirds are difficult to tell apart, it is usually a good idea to identify them by the generic name *Selasphorus* hummingbirds.

Anna's Hummingbird

Calypte anna

SIZE Medium-small (3.5–4 inches)

HABITAT Anna's Hummingbirds are found in suburban gardens, chaparral, and brushy oak woodlands. In cities in California and Arizona, this bird is often seen feeding on exotic plants and sugar-water feeders. In late summer many Anna's Hummingbirds move into the mountains to take advantage of abundantly blooming flowers.

OVERALL IMPRESSION The male Anna's often appears to have a solid rose-red head. Compared to similar hummingbirds, the Anna's seems a little chunky, and its underparts are more dingy.

CLAIM TO FAME The male Anna's has an iridescent helmet.

RANGE Anna's Hummingbirds occur regularly from southern British Columbia to southern California. They are also found in southern Arizona, and (to a lesser extent) in southern New Mexico, western and southern Nevada, and west Texas.

DESCRIPTION The male Anna's Hummingbird has bronze-green upperparts and dull gray underparts. His head and throat are an iridescent rose-red. A closer inspection will reveal that the bird has a broken white eye ring on its face, as well as white tips on an otherwise green tail. On the throat of the duller-plumaged female, there are numerous red or purple spangles that are often clustered together to form an irregular central blotch.

IDENTIFICATION TIP In some light conditions, the male's hood and throat may appear black or dark purple.

BEHAVIOR Early in the breeding season the male Anna's Hummingbird establishes a territory where there is a large supply of nectar-rich flowers. He chooses several perches from which he can sing and watch for intruders. When he sees other hummingbirds he will engage in elaborate flight displays or attempt to chase them away. In his display, the male Anna's Hummingbird will fly up 6 to 12 feet, then hover while making raspy sounds. The bird then ascends much higher before beginning a rapid descent directed toward either an unwelcome visitor or a female Anna's he is attempting to seduce. As this dive display is repeated over and over, the bird will orient himself so the sun will cause his red gorget to glitter.

When feeding from flowers or nectar feeders, the Anna's Hummingbird usually holds its tail stiff and straight down. The tail may wobble a bit, and occasionally it will wag more broadly.

A frequent singer, the Anna's Hummingbird can broadcast a raspy but surprisingly complex song.

NESTS Of all the birds in North America, Anna's Hummingbirds are probably the earliest to breed. Some Anna's Hummingbirds will be sitting on eggs before the first of the year. The female Anna's Hummingbird lays two white eggs in a woven cup she has constructed with tiny stems, plant down, and lichens. Nests have been found in a variety of habitats from two to thirty feet off the ground. The incubation period lasts about seventeen days. About twentyfive days later, the young leave the nest.

GENERAL COMMENTS If Anna's Hummingbirds are not normally expected in your area, but you think you have glimpsed a red-headed hummingbird at your feeder, be cautious about the identification. The red coloration of your feeder can reflect on a different hummingbird, creating the illusion that it is an Anna's.

Berylline Hummingbird

Amazilia beryllina

SIZE Medium (3.7–4 inches)

HABITAT Wooded mountain canyons.

OVERALL IMPRESSION A green hummingbird with a red bill.

CLAIM TO FAME Of all the hummingbird species that occur annually in the United States, the Berylline is the least common.

RANGE The Berylline Hummingbird is a rare summer resident in the mountains of southeastern Arizona. It also occasionally occurs in the mountains of southwestern New Mexico. This species has a large range in Mexico.

DESCRIPTION The male Berylline Hummingbird is emerald green on the back, head, and breast. Its wings and tail are rufous, and its beak is red at the base but black at the tip. The bird is cinnamon colored under the tail. The duller female has pale gray underparts.

IDENTIFICATION TIP There is no similar bird in its limited U.S. range.

BEHAVIOR This rare bird can be seen feeding or perched either low on flowers or high in trees.

NESTS Berylline Hummingbirds have been known to build nests in low shrubs as well as 20 or more feet off the ground in oaks, sycamores, and pines. The female puts together the nest using lichens and thin grasses, which she binds together with spiderwebs. Sometimes she leaves streamers—a few blades of grass—hanging down from the bottom. To make the nest more comfortable, she lines it with plant down. When the nest is nearly finished, she finds a mate and becomes fertilized. After that she lays two white eggs. Her young leave the nest about twenty days after they hatch.

GENERAL COMMENTS Since the northern edge of the breeding range of this species just barely reaches past the Arizona and New Mexico border, some Berylline Hummingbirds have difficulty finding a mate. As a result, our Berylline Hummingbirds sometimes either hybridize with other species or else abandon newly constructed nests. We once spent four days observing and videotaping a Berylline Hummingbird as it built a nest in the canyon above our home. We have vivid memories of her bill moving up and down like the needle of a sewing machine as she shaped a grayish-green cup on a branch of a small cherry tree. We held our breath as she gathered bits of lichen only 10 to 20 feet from the fallen log on which we were sitting. When the nest was almost complete she flew off to find a mate. That was the last we ever saw of her.

Black-chinned Hummingbird

Archilochus alexandri

SIZE Small (3.3–3.8 inches), but the females may have a relatively long bill.

HABITAT Woodlands, canyons with thickets, chaparral, mountain meadows, and orchards. In southwestern canyons males are most often found on relatively dry slopes, while females tend to choose nesting locations at lower, more verdant spots, usually over water and often in sycamore trees. In urban areas, Black-chins seem to prefer spaces with tall, flowering trees and an abundance of vines. At the northern end of their range, Black-chins often breed in residential areas and orchards. In California, Black-chinned Hummingbird nests are typically found in irrigated orchards and on the edge of agricultural land where there are trees.

OVERALL IMPRESSION The male is striking when sunlight catches the purple lower edge of its black gorget. The female is nondescript.

CLAIM TO FAME Widespread and common in a variety of habitats.

RANGE Black-chinned Hummingbirds breed across much of the western United States. Their range extends as far to the east as central Texas and as far to the north

as southern British Columbia. Most spend the winter in Mexico, but a few spend the cold months at feeders along the Gulf Coast from Texas to the Florida panhandle.

DESCRIPTION The Black-chinned is a small, slender hummingbird with a straight black bill. The adult male is bronze-green above. Its gorget is black with a metallic violet band on its lower edge. The female, green above and whitish or gray below, has a bill that is often slightly decurved and is longer than the bill of the male. Young Black-chins resemble adult females.

IDENTIFICATION TIPS Male Ruby-throats are occasionally mistaken for Black-chinned Hummingbirds, because —in certain lights —their throats can look quite black. But Ruby-throats never have a purple band across the lower edge of the gorget.

As a general rule, it is not wise to attempt to separate female Black-chinned Hummingbirds from female Ruby-throated Hummingbirds, unless the location and time of the sighting rules out one or the other. East Texas birds can reasonably be called Ruby-throats, and west Texas birds can reasonably be called Black-chins. In between, one must exert caution. Also, uncertainty can occur with out-of-season winter birds on the Gulf Coast of Louisiana and neighboring states, where out-of-range Black-chins are actually more likely than out-of-season Ruby-throats.

There are a few average differences between female Ruby-throats and female Black-chins that allow for an educated guess as to the species. The most useful difference is that female Black-chins tend to have longer bills. Also, the forehead of the Black-chinned is paler. Though it is not conclusive, Black-chinned Hummingbirds can often be separated from similar hummingbirds by the fact that they pump their tail almost constantly; it is as if there were a loose hinge where the tail connects to the body. Other similar hummingbirds may wag their tail, though rarely as often or as vigorously as the Black-chinned.

In the southwest, Black-chinned female and immature hummingbirds can be confused with female and immature Costa's Hummingbirds, which are smaller. The Costa's Hummingbird is also stockier and whiter beneath, and has a proportionally larger head and a shorter tail.

BEHAVIOR Black-chinned Hummingbirds are often seen chasing one another while making a twittering sound. Like other hummingbirds, they feed on flower nectar as well as small insects and spiders. Black-chinned Hummingbirds can be seen hunting for food anywhere from near the ground to the tops of trees. They are common feeder birds.

Though there are a few published reports of Black-chinned Hummingbirds singing a faint warbling sound, we have never heard it.

We have many times seen a male Black-chinned Hummingbird approach a perched female to do a zigzag aerial dance (or shuttle display) right in front of her face while she turns her head back and forth to watch him. Before awestruck females, males also do dive displays, which consist of a forward and backward aerial movement that follows the lower half of a large ellipse. The display is usually done 20 or 25 feet up in the air.

Black-chinned Hummingbirds are curious. We once saw one investigating a bright red male cardinal at such close range that we wondered if it mistook the bird for a red flower.

NESTS Black-chinned Hummingbirds usually build their nests in shrubs or small trees, where they anchor them on drooping branches. These nests are made of downy fibers and lichens, bound together with spiderwebs. In these tiny cups the female lays two white eggs. The incubation period is approximately thirteen to sixteen days, and fledglings leave the nest about twentytwo days after hatching.

GENERAL COMMENTS Though less colorful than other western species, the abundant and wide-ranging Black-chinned Hummingbird has been the subject of numerous research studies.

Blue-throated Hummingbird

Lampornis clemenciae

SIZE Large (4.8–5.3 inches)

HABITAT Wooded canyons.

RANGE Blue-throated Hummingbirds are found in the sycamore-lined canyons of southeastern Arizona, southwestern New Mexico, and west Texas. Typically these canyons have running water plus maple, madrone, pine, and juniper trees. The bird has a more extensive range in Mexico.

MIGRATION Blue-throats arrive in the United States in late March or early April, and most leave for Mexico by mid-October. A few stay all winter at feeders.

OVERALL IMPRESSION The Blue-throated Hummingbird is considerably larger than most other hummingbirds. It has a long tail and a unique azure-colored throat.

CLAIM TO FAME One of the two giant-sized hummingbirds in North America.

DESCRIPTION Blue-throated Hummingbirds have conspicuous white stripes above and below their dark cheeks. Their tails are large and expressive. The male has a blue throat, and the female is uniformly gray underneath.

IDENTIFICATION TIPS To quickly distinguish the female Blue-throated Hummingbird from the similar female Magnificent Hummingbird, one should first look at the tail. The Blue-throat exhibits bold patches of white when the tail flicks outward, while the Magnificent has only small white corners. Also, the Magnificent Hummingbird has a longer bill and doesn't flick its tail as boldly when feeding.

BEHAVIOR Blue-throats have the slowest wing beat of all the U.S. hummingbirds. They are often seen hovering in front of penstemons or thistle flowers near mountain streams. Blue-throated Hummingbirds dart out from exposed perches and zigzag erratically though canyon trees, repeatedly pausing midair to catch flying insects too small for humans eyes to see. These oversize hummingbirds also glean tiny insects and spiders from leaves, from the bark of trees, and from spiderwebs. Taking advantage of nature lovers who live in or near verdant mountain canyons, Blue-throated Hummingbirds eagerly take nectar from sugar-water feeders.

Endlessly fascinated by moving water, Blue-throated Hummingbirds often land on rocks in front of tiny waterfalls in mountain streams, where they fan out their wings and dip their bellies into the sparkling water. We have seen them do this even in the dead of winter. Blue-throats also like to hover in the delicate mist that spills out from these miniature rapids.

Blue-throats make a single-note call, often repeated over and over all day long. Like the cascading song of the Canyon Wren and the barking of Elegant Trogons, the monotonous peep of the Blue-throated Hummingbird is a signature sound of some of Arizona's most beautiful and verdant canyons near the Mexican border.

Blue-throats often duel with other members of their species, using swift, acrobatic movements. Sometimes two of them will collide in the air, thumping together, locking their bodies like wrestlers, then pecking at one another as they swirl down to the ground, kicking up a cloud of dust. One of the fighting hummingbirds may end up on its back as the other jabs it madly with its long beak. Finally the defeated hummingbird will fly off and yield the contested territory.

NESTS In Arizona the nests of Blue-throated Hummingbirds are often found on human structures, such as carports or porches. All they need is a ledge. We have seen them nest on top of a sheltered outdoor light fixture and on a decorative fishing net that was attached to the side of a building. Blue-throated Hummingbird nests have also been reported under rock overhangs, at the entrance to caves, and under the upper ledges of stream banks.

Blue-throats often return to the same spot where they nested the year before, building a new nest on top of an old one. We know of an abandoned shed that was, over a period of many years, used so many times that the stack of nests grew until it became about 2 inches wide and 18 inches high.

The female Blue-throat lays two white eggs, and then incubates them for about seventeen to eighteen days. The fledglings leave the nest about 24 to 29 days after hatching.

GENERAL COMMENTS Apparently a pre-Columbian culture had a special interest in this bird. There was an ancient Aztec god named Huitzilopochtli, a word that means "hummingbird on the left." In ceremonies the colors and patterns used in the costume of this warrior god were strongly reminiscent of a Blue-throated Hummingbird.

Blue-throated Hummingbirds are closely related to a group of hummingbirds in Latin America that are called Mountain-Gems.

RANGE OF ARIZONA SPECIALTY HUMMINGBIRDS

Broad-billed Hummingbird

Cynanthus latirostris

SIZE Medium-small (3.5–4 inches)

HABITAT Desert scrub and woodland areas, especially at the base of mountain canyons and along streambeds.

OVERALL IMPRESSION The body of the male is green, but its throat is blue. Both the male and the female have a red bill, though the red is less conspicuous on the female.

CLAIM TO FAME The glittering male of this species is a favorite of photographers.

RANGE Broad-bills are found in southeastern Arizona and southwestern New Mexico. They are occasionally found in the Big Bend area of southwestern Texas. These birds have a considerably more extensive range south of the border. Strays have appeared in southern California, Nevada, Utah, Louisiana, and Arkansas. Only an occasional bird remains in the United States in winter.

DESCRIPTION The male of this slender hummingbird species has a metallic green body that can sparkle like a precious stone with hundreds of facets. The bird's long, broad, bright-red bill is black at the tip. The deep blue coloration of the gorget does not have well-defined edges but blends into the green areas that surround it.

The female's bill is red-orange at the base and otherwise black. She is gray on the underparts and a deep green above. She has a gray patch behind the eye and usually shows a narrow white eye stripe above the patch.

Both the male and the female Broad-billed have a broad, wedge-shaped, blue-black tail that is notched. Both have a small, rounded head.

Juveniles resemble the female, though the young male may show green and blue flecks on the throat.

IDENTIFICATION TIPS In southeastern Arizona, female Broad-bills are often confused with female White-eared Hummingbirds, which are far less common. Keep in mind that the ear patch on a White-eared is black, not gray. Also, the White-eared has a shorter, straighter bill. And finally, the tail is forked on the Broad-billed, but cut straight across on the White-eared.

BEHAVIOR When they fly, Broad-billed Hummingbirds pump their large tails repeatedly. When approaching a feeder, they usually vocalize with a distinctive dry rattling sound. While interacting with other hummingbird species, Broad-billed Hummingbirds have been found to, as needed, change their foraging strategies or shift their position in the power structure.

NESTS The nests of Broad-billed Hummingbirds are constructed low to the ground, often near or over moving water. The nests, typically assembled from plant material that has washed up on the banks of streams, are usually built in vines or trees. Unlike other hummingbirds, Broad-bills rarely decorate their nests with lichens. Female Broad-bills lay two white eggs in a woven cup made of lichens and plant down. Incubation ranges from fourteen to seventeen days and is carried out by the female alone.

GENERAL COMMENTS While moving from flower to flower, Broad-billed Hummingbirds seem to hang like sequin-covered puppets on invisible strings.

Broad-tailed Hummingbird

Selasphorus platycercus

SIZE Medium-small (3.5–4 inches)

HABITAT The Broad-tailed Hummingbird breeds in the high country in the central and southern Rocky Mountains, where it is quite common in summer. This bird is especially abundant in subalpine meadows, in evergreen forests, on brushy slopes, and in pinyon-juniper woodlands.

OVERALL IMPRESSION The male Broad-tailed Hummingbird has a green back and a red throat, so he is superficially similar to the Ruby-throated Hummingbird. The female is green above and buff colored beneath.

CLAIM TO FAME The male makes a loud, buzzing trill when flying and is easily identified by this sound alone.

RANGE Broad-tails breed in the mountains from eastern California, Nevada, Idaho, and southwestern Montana through the Great Basin and Rocky Mountain states to Arizona, New Mexico, and western Texas. Their winter range is in Mexico.

DESCRIPTION The male Broad-tailed Hummingbird is bluish-green above; it has an iridescent red throat and gray underparts. His tail is long and, as his name implies, quite broad. The rufous coloration on the upper part of the tail may be difficult to see. The male Broad-tailed also has a white line from the chin to the white eye ring and then behind the eye to the neck. The female is green above and white washed with cinnamon beneath.

IDENTIFICATION TIPS Though male Broad-tails resemble male Ruby-throats, their ranges hardly ever overlap. The Broad-tailed has a much larger tail, and the red of its gorget is more of a rose color. The smaller tail of the Ruby-throated male is forked.

BEHAVIOR Broad-tails forage for flower nectar and insects in open meadows or in trees, where they may search as high as the mid-level.

The male's power display involves a steep climb to a point from 50 to almost 100 feet above the ground. There he hovers a moment, making wing trills before diving steeply, and then rising once again to form a U-shaped trajectory. Like several other hummingbirds, he also engages in shuttle and hovering displays.

NESTS In May or early June the female Broad-tailed lays two white eggs in a nest made of lichens, small roots, moss, and plant down. The outside of this rustic cradle is usually decorated with lichens or small shreds of bark. The nest, often constructed over a stream, can be as low as three feet above the ground, though sometimes it is considerably higher. The incubation period is about fifteen or sixteen days. Young leave the nest about twenty-three days after hatching.

GENERAL COMMENTS The male Broad-tailed is often heard before it is seen.

Buff-bellied Hummingbird

Amazilia yucatanensis

SIZE Medium (3.8–4.3 inches)

HABITAT Open woodlands, brushy areas, groves of citrus fruit trees.

OVERALL IMPRESSION A green hummingbird with a red bill and a buff-colored belly.

CLAIM TO FAME To see this bird you usually have to make a trip to the southernmost tip of Texas.

RANGE This hummingbird is common in the Rio Grande Valley and lower Texas coast from March to August. It is rare but regular in winter along the northern Gulf Coast from southern Texas to Florida. The Buff-bellied has a larger range along the east coast of Mexico.

DESCRIPTION Male and female Buff-bellied Hummingbirds are similar; their body is mostly bright green, but the belly is buff colored. The tail is reddish brown, and the red bill is black at the tip.

IDENTIFICATION TIPS This bird closely resembles the Berylline Hummingbird, but identification is not a problem, because the ranges of the two birds do not overlap.

BEHAVIOR These hummingbirds feed high and low from a wide variety of flowers, and they also glean insects. In south Texas they are often seen chasing away Ruby-throated and Black-chinned Hummingbirds from both flowers and feeders. During chases with other hummingbirds, the Buff-bellied commonly gives a rapid series of relatively low-pitched notes, all on the same pitch.

NESTS The female Buff-bellied Hummingbird lays two white eggs in a cup-shaped nest made of plant fibers and small pieces of bark. The outside of the nest is decorated with bark, lichens, and dried tree flowers, and the entire structure is bound together with spiderwebs. Buff-bellied nests are most often found in thickets or at the edge of a forest.

GENERAL COMMENTS This bird has been studied very little, so we still have much to learn about it.

RANGE OF BUFF-BELLIED HUMMINGBIRD

Calliope Hummingbird

Stellula calliope

SIZE Very small (3–3.2 inches)

HABITAT The Calliope Hummingbird spends its summers in the cool, sometimes cold northern Rockies as well as in the high Sierras of California. This petite bird is most often seen in evergreen forests and mountain meadows. It is the hummingbird most likely to be encountered at or above the timberline. In migration, Calliopes are seen in a wide range of habitats.

OVERALL IMPRESSION Calliopes have a very short bill and tail. The males have candy-striped gorgets.

CLAIM TO FAME Our smallest hummingbird.

RANGE The Calliope Hummingbird breeds from central British Columbia and southwestern Alberta through Washington state and eastern Oregon to northern California, the Sierras, and northern Nevada. It also breeds in Idaho, western Wyoming, and Utah. Almost all Calliopes spend the winter in central Mexico, but a few are seen every winter at feeders along the northern Gulf Coast.

Most Calliopes migrate up the Pacific Coast in spring, though some migrate through Arizona and western New Mexico. The first Calliopes arrive in southern California in early March, but they usually don't reach Oregon until early May. In Idaho and Montana, Calliopes may not arrive before mid- or late May.

Calliope Hummingbirds depart from their breeding grounds sometime between midsummer and late August. Most take a more easterly route to get back to Mexico after the breeding season. As a result, many migrating Calliopes can be seen passing through Arizona and western New Mexico in late summer and early fall.

Range of Calliope Hummingbird

DESCRIPTION The male Calliope is quite striking with his shaggy beard that may appear to be solidly magenta colored when seen from a distance, but streaked with long magenta and white lines when seen at a closer range. Sometimes the reddish streaks flare out against their white background to make a starlike formation. The male's upper breast is white. His back, nape, and the top of his head are green.

The female Calliope has no gorget, but her throat may show some speckling. On her back and on the top of her head she is green, and she has a rusty wash on her cream-colored underparts.

Calliope Hummingbirds have short bills and short tails. When they are perched on a feeder, their wings extend a short distance beyond the end of the slightly notched tail. Both males and females can show some rufous coloration at the base of the tail.

IDENTIFICATION TIPS The female Calliope Hummingbird can be confused with small, drab females of a few other western species, especially female and immature Rufous Hummingbirds. With a pair of binoculars one can carefully examine the relative length of the bill, the wings, and the tail. If the tail extends beyond the wings, the bird is not a Calliope.

BEHAVIOR Being small, the Calliope Hummingbird is at a disadvantage when competing with other species of hummingbirds. Nevertheless, this tiny bird can be quite aggressive when diving at Broad-tailed and Black-chinned Hummingbirds, and the female has been known to dive-bomb human intruders who are near her nest. In summer, Calliopes don't have much competition because they nest at higher elevations than other hummingbirds. During migration, Calliopes often survive competition from larger hummingbirds by foraging close to the ground on the bottommost flowers rather than the middle and uppermost flowers where other hummingbirds tend to go. When Calliopes are passing through our area we often hang a feeder or two on low branches.

During the breeding season the male Calliope sometimes engages in a dive display during which he first rises about 80 feet in the air, and then swoops down, making a loud whistle. Finally he swoops back up again. As this aerial maneuver is repeated, he etches a huge letter U in the air. Male Calliopes also engage in another, less elaborate display in which they first hover about 30 feet in the air, then dive at intruders.

NESTS Calliope nests are usually under a protective branch at the eastern edge of a wooded area where the early morning sun will quickly warm them up. The nests, often hidden in clusters of pinecones, can be as low as 2 feet off the ground or as high as 70 feet. They are constructed with bark shreds, moss, willow-seed filaments, lichens, pine needles, insect cocoons, and spider silk. After insulating the nest with downy materials, the female lays two white eggs, and then she spends a great deal of time sitting on them until they hatch. When the young come out of their shells, she continues to brood them until they develop enough feathers to keep warm. The incubation period is seventeen to twentytwo days, and the fledglings leave the nest about twentytwo days after hatching.

GENERAL COMMENTS In classical mythology, Calliope was the muse of heroic poetry. The genus name for this species is Stellula, which means "little star" and probably refers to the way the male's gorget looks when it is fanned out.

The Calliope Hummingbird is the smallest hummingbird in the United States, but not the smallest hummingbird in the world. That honor goes to the Bee Hummingbird of Cuba.

Costa's Hummingbird

Calypte costae

SIZE Small (3–3.4 inches)

HABITAT This bird breeds in open areas of desert scrub, especially in washes where there is ocotillo. It is also associated with desert areas characterized by sage, Joshua tree, or cholla cactus.

OVERALL IMPRESSION The entire head of the male looks purple, and the lower ends of the gorget flare out with long purple tails. The female is nondescript.

CLAIM TO FAME Like the Anna's Hummingbird, the male Costa's Hummingbird has an iridescent helmet—though not the same color.

RANGE The Costa's Hummingbird is seen year-round in southern California and southwestern Arizona. In the breeding season it also occurs in central California; western and southern Nevada; and much of western, central, and southern Arizona. In summer, members of this species can be seen as far east as the New Mexico boot heel.

DESCRIPTION The male Costa's Hummingbird has a long, light-purple gorget and a helmet that is the same striking color. This green-backed bird has pale gray underparts and dull green flanks. The female and immature birds are green above and pale gray underneath, and their white throats are sometimes speckled with purple.

IDENTIFICATION TIPS Females and immatures can easily be confused with Black-chinned Hummingbirds, which are slimmer and have longer bills and tails. When perched, the Black-chin's tail extends beyond the wing tips, while the tip of the tail of the Costa's Hummingbird doesn't extend quite as far as the end of the wings. Also, the Costa's gives a different call note.

Female Costa's Hummingbirds can also be confused with female Anna's. The Anna's are noticeably larger and stockier. The tail of the female Anna's is more square-shaped and she is more dingy underneath.

BEHAVIOR The male Costa's does a display in which he flies about 80 feet up, then, while making shrill whistles, he engages in a power dive with his gorget and helmet oriented toward the sun. After looping past a potential mate, he soars back up for another power dive. This is repeated several times.

NESTS Costa's Hummingbirds nest very early. The breeding season is usually from mid-February to June. The female lays two white eggs in a delicate-looking nest that is decorated on the outside with leaves or lichens. Often the nest is assembled on a low, sheltered branch of a bush or small tree. Some of these birds build their nests on yucca stalks. To the delight of many homeowners, female Costa's Hummingbirds are often attracted to outdoor patios, where they have been known to build nests atop wind chimes. The incubation period for this bird is from fifteen to eighteen days, and the young leave the nest about twenty to twentythree days after hatching.

GENERAL COMMENTS The Costa's Hummingbird was named after a French noble-man whose full name is Louis Marie Pantaleon Costa, Marquis de Beauregard.

Lucifer Hummingbird

Calothorax lucifer

SIZE Medium-small (3.5–4 inches long), but with a long, decurved bill.

HABITAT Chihuahuan desert and nearby foothills where there are agaves; dry canyons and arroyos.

OVERALL IMPRESSION The male has an oversize, deep-purple gorget. Both the male and the female have a distinctly arched bill.

CLAIM TO FAME Difficult to find.

RANGE Southeastern Arizona and extreme southwestern New Mexico; also, the Big Bend area of Texas. The range of the Lucifer Hummingbird is limited in the United States but large in Mexico. The Lucifer Hummingbirds that establish breeding-season territories north of the border usually arrive in April and are gone by early October.

DESCRIPTION This small hummingbird has a thin body and relatively short wings.

Its bill is long and noticeably curved. The green-backed adult male has a large gorget that is a metallic magenta or violet-purple. His bronze-green flanks are mixed with cinnamon and give the bird the appearance that it is wearing a vest. The male Lucifer has a deeply forked tail; but, when he is perched at a feeder, his folded tail is so thin it may appear to be nothing more than a single long, narrow feather.

The female Lucifer is green above and she has cinnamon underparts. Her long, wide eye stripe curves downward as it approaches her neck. Immature Lucifers are similar to adult female Lucifers.

When vocalizing, Lucifer Hummingbirds make a shrill, squeaky chirp note that can be learned with practice. In flight the male may make a low-pitched whirring sound.

MORE IDENTIFICATION TIPS Beginners who have never seen a female Lucifer often think they have found one when they see either a female Black-chinned or a female Costa's Hummingbird, both of which can have a relatively long and slightly decurved bill. The female Lucifer can be distinguished, however, by the distinctly cinnamon wash on her underparts and also by her long, wide eye stripe. In addition, the bill of the female Lucifer is considerably more arched than the bill of a Black-chin or Costa's.

Though immature male Lucifers can resemble immature male Calliopes, the Lucifer's bill and tail are longer.

BEHAVIOR Unlike other male hummingbirds, the Lucifer Hummingbird often does a courtship display at the nest of a female. This may occur as she engages in building the nest and even when she sits on eggs. In courtship the male zigzags in front of the female and then flies high in the sky before diving precipitously.

Lucifer Hummingbirds often feed on leftover nectar in agave flowers where bats may have feasted during the previous night. Because the bats help pollinate the agaves but the Lucifers do not, one researcher has called the Lucifer a nectar thief.

NESTS The breeding season for the Lucifer Hummingbird is from April to August. The Lucifer female usually selects a low place on a cholla cactus, an agave, or an ocotillo as a place to build a nest made of plant fibers, down, and lichens. She uses spiderwebs to bind the nest together and decorates the outside with small leaves or lichen flakes. After the female lays two long, white, elliptical eggs, she incubates them for a little more than two weeks. The young then hatch and stay in the nest for twenty to twenty-four days.

GENERAL COMMENTS The word Lucifer has no satanic implications. It literally means "light bearer." Though this is one of the most difficult hummingbirds to find in the United States, we know of a private home in a remote canyon in the Peloncillo Mountains of New Mexico where, all through the breeding season, numerous Lucifer Hummingbirds are easily seen at sugar-water feeders. Unfortunately, the road to this secluded homestead passes through another ranch that does not allow traffic from outside visitors. The best places to try to see Lucifer Hummingbirds are in southeastern Arizona in the wooded canyons south of Sierra Vista; in Patagonia; in Portal; and in Madera Canyon, which is west of Green Valley.

Magnificent Hummingbird

Eugenes fulgens

SIZE Large (4.7–5.3 inches)

HABITAT Dry pine-oak mountain forests; wooded canyons.

OVERALL IMPRESSION A very large, dark hummingbird.

CLAIM TO FAME One of the two giant-size hummingbirds that are regularly seen in the United States.

RANGE Magnificent Hummingbirds are found in the mountains of southeastern Arizona, southwestern New Mexico, and west Texas. The bird also has an extensive range in the mountains of Mexico. Most U.S. Magnificents go south in fall, but a few linger all winter at nectar feeders, especially in southeastern Arizona.

DESCRIPTION The male Magnificent is so dark that some people call it the black knight. As the bird moves about it may show glittering bits of color on the throat and the helmet. With better light and sun orientation one can see that the iridescent throat of this appropriately named bird is lime green and that the crown is purple. With excellent light, the bird has a metallic luster like the brightest of Christmas tree ornaments. The bill of the Magnificent Hummingbird is unusually long, and the bird has a white dot behind its eye. Scruffy-looking immature males have the same color pattern, but they are less boldly colored.

The female Magnificent is similar to the male, but she lacks the iridescent green and purple feathers the male has on the crown and throat. Her underparts are gray, and her bill is, like the bill of the male, unusually long.

Both the male and the female hover with their back held perpendicular to the ground, and both exhibit small white corners on the tail. When they land on a feeder they often curl their tail forward as they lap up sugar-water while their long, straight bills force their heads to tilt back from the feeding ports.

These large hummingbirds vocalize with a sharp chirp that is not always on the same pitch. They also emit rapid whining and crackling sounds when in a chase.

IDENTIFICATION TIP To separate female Magnificents from similar-sized female Blue-throated Hummingbirds, look above to the identification tips for Blue-throats.

BEHAVIOR Magnificent Hummingbirds like to perch on open branches where they can dart out to catch flying insects. To gather nectar from a large variety of flowers, they also venture out a fair distance in various directions.

Though they can be aggressive at times, Magnificent Hummingbirds are often chased away by other more domineering species, such as Blue-throated and Rufous Hummingbirds.

NESTS Using a tree branch, often one that hangs over a stream, the female Magnificent builds a relatively large nest that consists of plant materials and moss. The nest is lined with plant down and decorated on the outside with lichens. There will be two white eggs, which will be incubated for approximately fifteen to nineteen days. The young will leave the nest about twentyfive days later.

GENERAL COMMENTS This bird was formerly called the Rivoli's Hummingbird.

Though we sometimes refer to Magnificent and Blue-throated Hummingbirds as "giant" hummingbirds, there is a hummingbird in South America, aptly called the Giant Hummingbird, that is considerably bigger that either of them. The Giant Hummingbird is 8.5 inches long.

Ruby-throated Hummingbird

Archilochus colubris

SIZE Small (3.2–3.7 inches)

HABITAT Woodlands, orchards, parks, gardens.

OVERALL IMPRESSION The male is green with a red throat. The female is green above and pale gray underneath.

CLAIM TO FAME This is the best-known hummingbird in the United States.

RANGE The Ruby-throated Hummingbird occurs in all states east of the Great Plains. The breeding range extends as far west as east Texas and much of Oklahoma, plus eastern sections of Nebraska, Kansas, and the Dakotas. Ruby-throats do not nest in southern Florida, but can be seen there during migration and occasionally in winter. In southern Canada, Ruby-throated Hummingbirds establish territories and nest annually all the way from the eastern coast to south-central Alberta. No other hummingbird nests east of the Mississippi River. Ruby-throated Hummingbirds spend the winter in Central America and southern Mexico. Occasionally, a few

Ruby-throats will spend the winter in southern Florida or on the northern Gulf Coast.

From March through May, Ruby-throated Hummingbirds migrate north, some through the eastern two-thirds of Texas, some through Cuba and Florida, and many directly across the Gulf of Mexico. Migrating birds reach the southern Gulf Coast in late February and early March. The latest migrating birds are the ones that will fly the farthest north. Late-summer departure time usually corresponds with the end of the blooming season for food plants. Fall migration lasts from late July in northern areas until late October in the deep South.

RANGE OF RUBY-THROATED HUMMINGBIRD

DESCRIPTION The male Ruby-throat has a brilliant red throat and a black chin. Greenish above and whitish below, he appears to be wearing a slightly opened vest. The tail is forked. Female Ruby-throats and the immature birds of this species are greenish above and grayish white beneath.

IDENTIFICATION TIPS In certain lights, the gorget of the male Ruby-throat will appear to be black or green. Unaware that a male Black-chinned Hummingbird would show a purple band on the lower edge of its gorget, backyard bird-watchers in the East sometimes mistakenly think they have seen a Black-chinned Hummingbird at their feeder when what they have actually seen is a Ruby-throat with a darkened gorget.

RANGE The range of the Black-chinned Hummingbird and the Ruby-throated Hummingbird can overlap in the Great Plains, in central Texas, and on the Gulf Coast in winter. As a general rule, female Black-chins have longer bills and pump their tail much more vigorously than Ruby-throats, but this is not 100 percent diagnostic. For most people most of the time, it would be wise to call uncertain females or immatures by the generic name—*Archilochus.*

BEHAVIOR Ruby-throated Hummingbirds sometimes arrive on their breeding grounds before any flowers are blooming. They survive by eating insects and also by gathering sap from holes drilled in trees by woodpeckers. As soon as flowers start blooming—or if they are already blooming—males establish territories. To defend their quarter-acre kingdoms against intruders, males do tail spreading, shuttle displays, and vertical face-to-face flights. When females arrive they, too, establish a territory and make these same displays. One display made by the male but not the female is a dive during which he flies in a U-shaped trajectory, rising ten or more feet on either end.

NESTS The difficult-to-find nests of Ruby-throated Hummingbirds are made of plant down, supplemented with bits of lichens and bud scales. These nests are usually constructed on small, downward-sloping branches that are covered with lichens. Both deciduous and coniferous trees are used. The average height of a Ruby-throat's nest is about 15 feet above the ground, but it can be lower or considerably higher. The most likely places to find these nests are at the edges of forest clearings, by streams, or in the trees along the edge of a road.

When the nest is completed, the female Ruby-throat lays two eggs. The incubation period is about sixteen days. After about nineteen days of being fed in the nest, the young hop out of the nest and take their first flight. In the warmer, more southern parts of the breeding range, there are often two broods in a single summer.

GENERAL COMMENTS Many Ruby-throated Hummingbirds annually fly across the Gulf of Mexico, although it's not the only route to and from their wintering grounds. This is one of the most remarkable feats of nature.

Rufous Hummingbird

Selasphorus rufus

SIZE Small (3.2–3.7 inches)

HABITAT Forest, woodland edges, thickets. Migrants can be abundant in a variety of habitats.

OVERALL IMPRESSION The orange-gold male Rufous Hummingbird is dazzling. Females and immature birds are greenish above and whitish beneath, usually tinted here and there with rufous coloration.

CLAIM TO FAME The Rufous Hummingbird has the longest migration route of any hummingbird.

RANGE The Rufous Hummingbird breeds in southern Alaska and western Canada. It also breeds in Washington state, Oregon, Idaho, western Montana, and some of the northernmost regions of California.

In migration this bird is commonly seen throughout the west. Spring migrants are more common in states that border the Pacific Ocean; they pass through

California from February to May. Birds reach Alaska by mid-April and they reach Montana by late April or early May. Fall migrants commonly appear in California in late June, July, and August. In late summer and fall, Rufous Hummingbird migrants also can be abundant in the interior west. From mid-July through August, Rufous Hummingbirds can be common in Colorado. They are often common in Arizona, New Mexico, and west Texas in late summer, especially August, and many linger into September.

Though most Rufous Hummingbirds spend the winter in Mexico, a few regularly winter at feeders and flower gardens along the northern Gulf Coast from Texas to Florida. Though rare, wintering Rufous Hummingbirds have been recorded in almost every eastern state and even at a few locations in southern Canada.

RANGE OF RUFOUS HUMMINGBIRD

DESCRIPTION The body of an adult male Rufous Hummingbird is solid orange-gold; his gorget is an iridescent copper-red. The beak is black, and his wings are relatively short. When the male Rufous Hummingbird flies, he often makes a whirring noise that is similar to but softer than the flight noise of a male Broad-tailed Hummingbird.

The back and the top of the head on a female Rufous Hummingbird are green but flecked with rufous. Her throat can be clear or streaked with bronze-green. Her tail is rufous at the base, then green, black, and white. The immature resembles the female, but immature males may have a spangled blotch of color on the throat. Immature Rufous Hummingbirds often have at least some orange-red coloration mixed in with their green plumage.

When coming to feeders, Rufous Hummingbirds often emit a fairly loud chirp note.

MORE IDENTIFICATION TIPS The very similar adult male Allen's Hummingbirds are green rather than rufous on the upper back, while adult male Rufous Hummingbirds almost always show no green patch on the back. Nevertheless, about 1 to 2 percent of all adult male Rufous Hummingbirds also have a green back. Therefore, in areas where the two species overlap, the only totally safe identification is an adult male Rufous Hummingbird with no green on its back.

It is, for all practical purposes, impossible to separate female and immature Allen's Hummingbirds from Rufous females and immatures. One can either call them by the generic name, *Selasphorus,* or else label them Rufous/Allen's.

Immature male Rufous Hummingbirds are often misidentified as Allen's Hummingbirds. If the bird does not have a full gorget, resist the temptation to identify the genus; stick with the generic name.

In most cases the only time there is certainty about the separation of Allen's and Rufous Hummingbirds is when a licensed expert captures the bird and examines the tail feathers. A limited number of bird banders and ornithologists have permission from the federal government to do this.

BEHAVIOR The Rufous Hummingbird is small but fierce. As many frustrated backyard bird-watchers have found, it can chase away every other hummingbird in sight.

When a male Rufous Hummingbird senses an intruder in his territory—and also when he is courting a female—he engages in displays. The bird may fan out his rufous tail or spread his gorget. He may engage in a shuttle flight or a more elaborate dive display, during which he moves through the air in a lopsided oval trajectory. On the downward side of the oval, his wings may make a whining, rattling sound.

NESTS The female Rufous Hummingbird usually builds a nest in a sheltered place in a shrub or conifer. Sometimes several will nest in close proximity to one another. The nest is a soft, cottony cup, surrounded by moss and spiderwebs, then camouflaged on the outside with lichen flakes or small pieces of bark. The complete nest is about two inches wide and one-and-a-half inches deep. Two white, jelly bean–shaped eggs are laid sometime between mid-April and mid-July and incubated by the female for about seventeen days. The young leave the nest about twenty days after hatching.

GENERAL COMMENTS It can be frustrating when a migrating Rufous Hummingbird shows up in your backyard to claim all your feeders as its own exclusive property, never to be shared. It may spend days or weeks chasing off every other hummingbird that enters your yard. Sometimes it seems the Rufous is wasting more energy chasing hummers away than it is gaining from the nectar feeders. All Rufous Hummingbirds are not this aggressive, but many are.

One solution may be to space the feeders so that the Rufous can't see all of them. One or more feeders may, for example, be placed around the corner of a house. Another strategy may be to cluster several feeders together, making it impossible for the hummingbird to defend all of them at the same time. Also, when large swarms of hummingbirds are passing through, total exclusionary rights may be a task it is simply not able to keep up with.

Violet-crowned Hummingbird

Amazilia violiceps

SIZE Medium-large (4–4.5 inches)

HABITAT Violet-crowned Hummingbirds are uncommon to rare in areas south and east of Tucson. These handsome birds can be found in extreme southwestern New Mexico. The most likely place to find Violet-crowns is at the mouths of canyons, where a line of sycamores, cottonwoods, and willows follow an emerging creek.

OVERALL IMPRESSION The Violet-crowned Hummingbird is easy to identify. It has a straight, bright red bill, and its white underparts usually look immaculate.

CLAIM TO FAME Violet-crowns are striking and beautiful, even though they don't have a gorget.

RANGE Southeastern Arizona and southwestern New Mexico. The bird has a much more extensive range in Mexico. Typically birds in the United States leave in fall, but occasionally a few will stay all winter at feeding stations.

DESCRIPTION Males and females are similar. The crown is bluish violet while the back and tail are grayish-greenish brown. The bill is bright red with a black tip. The throat and underparts are white. The tail is squared and has no white. Immatures are similarly colored but duller.

IDENTIFICATION TIP The Violet-crowned Hummingbird does not resemble any other North American hummingbird.

BEHAVIOR Violet-crowns lap up nectar, especially from flowers in the trees. They glean insects from foliage and out of the air.

Violet-crowns give a distinctive dry, loud call note, either singly or in a rattled series. Though there is little scientific information about their song, we once sat at a picnic table and heard a Violet-crowned Hummingbird singing from a perch that was only five feet way. Each time the bird opened its long, red bill, its immaculate white throat swelled and vibrated, producing a song that was complex and surprisingly musical—at least for the part we could hear. About half the song was completely inaudible to us, because the frequency was too high. It was as if we were watching television and periodically pressing the mute button.

NESTS In the United States the Violet-crowned Hummingbird breeds from April to September. Nests are usually in sycamore trees, often near the tip of a horizontal branch. The nest is made primarily of white, cottony plant down that has been bound together with spiderwebs. Its exterior is often decorated with lichens and weed seeds.

GENERAL COMMENTS For many years a Violet-crowned Hummingbird has nested every July on a low-hanging branch of a large sycamore in front of the Portal, Arizona, post office and library. This is just above the place where numerous cars frequently pull in, park, and then pull back out again. It is also where most of the town gossip takes place.

White-eared Hummingbird

Hylocharis leucotis

SIZE Medium-small (3.5–4 inches)

HABITAT Usually found in pine-oak woodlands near mountain streams.

OVERALL IMPRESSION The male has a dark head with a bold white eye stripe. He also has a bright red bill.

CLAIM TO FAME Beautiful and rare.

RANGE The White-eared hummingbird is a Mexican species whose summer range extends north just past the border. Most sightings are in southeastern Arizona, but the bird has been seen in New Mexico and west Texas.

DESCRIPTION The male of this species has a long white eye stripe that extends over and above his black ear patch. His bill is straight and bright red; the tip is black. The tail of the male White-eared is broad, squared, and slightly cleft. His upper-parts and his throat are iridescent green; his head is a metallic blue-violet; his belly is white and his underparts are spotted with green. The duller female White-eared Hummingbird has a long white eye line like the male, but her ear patch is dusky, not boldly black. Her bill is red at the base.

IDENTIFICATION TIPS The female White-eared can be separated from the more common female Broad-billed Hummingbird by her light gray throat that is speckled with green—and also by her tail and flanks, which are greenish.

BEHAVIOR The White-eared Hummingbird feeds from the mid-level of trees down to flowers that are blooming on the ground. The male sometimes sings from hidden perches deep inside of trees.

NESTS After selecting a site in a shrub or a tree, usually 5 to 20 feet off the ground, the female White-eared constructs a nest using plant materials, moss, pine needles, and spider webs. She covers the nest with lichens and moss, and lines it with plant down. She lays two white eggs, and then incubates them for about fifteen days before they hatch.

GENERAL COMMENTS Most White-eared Hummingbird sightings are in the wooded canyons of the Huachuca Mountains, which are just south of Sierra Vista, Arizona. The next most likely places are in the nearby Chiricahua and Santa Rita Mountains.

CHAPTER THREE

VAGRANTS, ALBINOS, AND HYBRIDS

Vagrant Hummingbirds

The following hummingbirds occur less than once a year in the United States:

Bahama Woodstar *Calliphlox evelynae*
Small (3.4–3.7 inches)

There are just a few records of this small hummingbird. All are from south Florida. The bird's deeply forked tail is long, extending well beyond the wings when at rest. The male is green above and has a magenta-rose gorget; its sides are cinnamon. The tail is blackish with rufous-colored inner webs.

Bumblebee Hummingbird *Atthis heloisa*
Very small (2.7–3 inches)

Two specimens of this very small hummingbird were collected in Arizona's Huachuca Mountains in 1896. There have been no other reports. The male has a shaggy, magenta-rose gorget and a rufous base to the tail. The slightly larger Calliope Hummingbird can easily be mistaken for a Bumblebee Hummingbird, especially if the male's red throat is seen from a distance and appears to have a solid-colored gorget.

Cinnamon Hummingbird *Amazilia rutila*
Medium (4–4.5 inches)

This medium-large hummingbird is plain green on the head and upperparts. The bill is mostly red, and the underparts are cinnamon. There is one record for Arizona and one for New Mexico.

Cuban Emerald *Chlorostilbon ricordii*
Medium (3.7–4.2 inches)

This small hummingbird has been seen several times in south Florida.

It has a long, deeply forked tail. The male is green overall and has some red coloration on the bill.

Green-breasted Mango *Anthracothorax prevostii*
Medium-large (4.5–4.8 inches)

There are a few autumn and winter records for this larger-than-average hummingbird—all in south Texas and none farther north than Corpus Christi. The male is green overall and has a purple tail. The female has a conspicuous dark line running down the entire center of her whitish underparts.

Green-breasted Mango

Green Violet-ear *Colibri thalassinus*
Medium-large (4.2–4.7 inches)

For reasons no one understands, this medium-size hummingbird has, on numerous occasions, wandered far north of its normal range in Mexico and Central America. This bird has appeared mostly in Texas but also at scattered locations across the eastern United States. There is even a record of Green Violet-ear for Ontario, Canada. This dark bird is green overall, but it has a violet ear patch and a bluish-purple patch on the chest. A dark band goes across the tail.

Green Violet-ear

Plain-capped Starthroat *Heliomaster constantii*
Medium with very long bill (4.7–5 inches)

Of all the birds we have classified as vagrants, the Starthroat is the one most likely to occur in the United States. Numerous records exist for southeastern Arizona. We once had the good fortune of seeing one a short ways upstream from our house site.

This medium-size hummingbird is bronze-green on the back and on the top of the head; the underparts are pale gray. The throat is red or

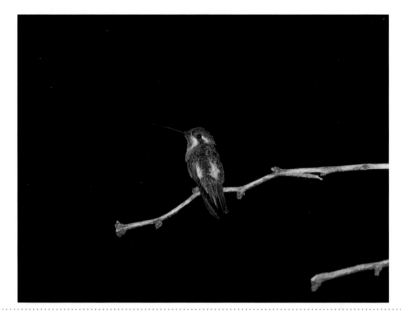

Plain-capped Starthroat

gray-brown. The tail is green with white corners and a black terminal band. There is a black stripe over the eye, and the bird has a long bill. When it perches, it often shows white fluffs coming out from under its wings. Though most U.S. records have been at feeders, the bird seems to particularly enjoy feeding from agaves.

Xantus' Hummingbird *Basilinna xantusii*
Small (3.3–3.8 inches)

The Xantus is a medium to small hummingbird, which has, on a couple of occasions, wandered north to southern California. It has a thick white stripe behind the eye that contrasts strongly with the black ear patch. The bird is cinnamon colored below and green above. It has a red bill, and the tail is mostly reddish brown.

Albino Hummingbirds

The first time we saw a white hummingbird was in the backyard of a Baptist preacher in southern Louisiana in a small town on the north shore of Lake Pontchartrain. He insisted on calling the tiny bird a white angel. After receiving a phone call, we drove two hours to see it. Fortunately for us, the bird was there when we arrived. Though it was a little larger and heavier than the norm, the bird was identified as a Ruby-throat. It was

Leucistic Hummingbird

surprisingly aggressive, chasing away every other hummingbird in sight. With other white hummingbirds we have seen since then, the situation has been reversed: Much to the chagrin of people trying to get a good look, the normal-looking hummingbirds repeatedly chased away the albinos.

Complete albino hummingbirds with pure white plumage, red eyes, pink bills, and pink feet are hardly ever seen. Leucistic hummingbirds are more likely. These have whitish plumage washed with a pale yellowish brown or gray coloring. The bills and feet of leucistic hummingbirds can be normal in coloration or pale. It is also possible to see a partial albino hummingbird that has patches of normal color and also patches of white. On one occasion, we had a white hummingbird come to our own feeders in the Chiricahua Mountains. It was a leucistic Black-chinned Hummingbird.

Hybrid Hummingbirds

Hummingbirds hybridize more than most other birds. This may be partially explained by the fact that hummingbirds do not form pair bonds, and partly by the fact that the hummingbird males hardly ever take part in the building of nests or the care of nestlings and fledglings.

Many mixes of different species are possible. Occasionally a hummingbird will even copulate and produce hybrid offspring with a member of another species of hummingbird that is different in size, plumage, and preferred habitat. The progeny of such interspecies unions usually share blended characteristics of the two parents, but not always.

CHAPTER FOUR

IDENTIFYING HUMMINGBIRDS

In this chapter we offer five considerations to take into account when trying to identify an unfamiliar hummingbird.

1. Is It Really a Hummingbird?

This is a more important question than most people realize. It is common for gardeners to see winged creatures feeding from flowers and then incorrectly identify them as hummingbirds. Sphinx moths or hawk moths often act just like hummingbirds, hovering, dipping in for nectar, flying back out again while still facing the flowers. These hummingbirdlike moths often visit nectar feeders just as hummingbirds do, and they have long proboscises that can be mistaken for the bills of hummingbirds.

Sphinx Moth

At the Hummingbird Web Site (www.hummingbirdworld.com) we frequently receive e-mails inquiring about tiny "hummingbirds" with rings around their bodies. Often these sightings are at dusk. Invariably these turn out to be moths. So how does one tell a hummingbird from a moth? Here are some suggestions:

- Hummingbirds are never active at night. Moths can be active both at night and during the day.
- Moths have long, feathered antennae on their foreheads. Hummingbirds do not have antennae.
- Moths have segmented bodies, as do other insects. Hummingbirds do not.
- Moths often have markings no hummingbird would have. No North American hummingbird, for example, has rings around its neck or body, but many moths do.
- Half-grown hummingbirds are not capable of flight. Hummingbirds do not leave the nest until they are nearly full size. "Baby hummingbirds" feeding in flower gardens are probably moths.
- Moths may have color patterns that no hummingbird would have.

Two of the more common hummingbirdlike moths are the snowberry clearwing hummingbird moth and the tersa sphinx hummingbird moth. In Arizona we frequently see another, the white-lined sphinx moth, which has many bands and stripes, some white, some pinkish. Our sphinx moths feed in our hummingbird garden and at our nectar feeders, just as our hummingbirds do.

Don't be disappointed when you discover that you have been watching a moth rather than a hummingbird. Moths are delightful little creatures, well worth our attention.

2. Location

It matters a great deal where a hummingbird is seen. If you live in the eastern half of the United States and see a hummingbird in your summer flower garden, the odds are about 100 percent that the bird is a Ruby-throat. Many e-mails have come in to the Hummingbird

Web Site reporting Black-chinned Hummingbirds in Eastern states during the breeding season. For all practical purposes, this is impossible. In certain lights the throat of a male Ruby-throated Hummingbird looks black. One can see a male Ruby-throat repeatedly without ever realizing that the true color of the throat is red.

Sometimes location is a dead giveaway: A hummingbird seen in Alaska is going to be a Rufous Hummingbird. No other hummingbird travels that far north. A "hummingbird" seen in Hawaii or Europe is going to be a figment of one's imagination, because hummingbirds do not naturally occur in either of those locations.

At many locations in the West, two or three species of hummingbird are possible. This knowledge allows one to quickly narrow down the choices.

Throughout much of the West, the most common hummingbird is the Black-chinned, but others can be more common in particular areas and at particular times of the year. In spring and fall migration, the Rufous Hummingbird may be the most common. In coastal California, the Anna's Hummingbird and the Allen's Hummingbird are common, but migrating Rufous Hummingbirds can be common, too. The Costa's Hummingbird may be regular in desert areas of southern California and southwestern Arizona. In the Rocky Mountains, the common hummingbirds may be the Broad-tailed and the Calliope. The Rufous Hummingbird is common in summer in western Canada. In the Rio Grande Valley of Texas you might see a Buff-bellied Hummingbird. The Allen's Hummingbird is rarely seen outside of California, and you should use extreme caution in identifying it in any other state.

The only places where one might be overwhelmed by possibilities are in the mountains of southeastern Arizona, southwestern New Mexico, and western Texas. At our home in the Chiricahua Mountains we have seen as many as 11 species in a single day, and we have seen 15 species within two miles of our home.

A couple of extremely rare species of hummingbird are possible in the Florida Keys. These are the Cuban Emerald and the Bahama Woodstar. Your chances of seeing them are slim, even if you live there and watch hummingbirds regularly.

Most of the United States and southern Canada has at least one type of nesting hummingbird. In some parts of the Great Plains, however, hummingbirds are seen only as occasional visitors during migration. Hummingbirds are also absent in southern Florida in the summertime.

3. What Season Is It?

The nesting season for hummingbirds is usually June and July, though some nest considerably earlier. Spring migration for most species is from March through May (though Allen's Hummingbirds migrate much earlier.) Migration back south is usually from mid-July to October. Migration season in northern regions tends to be at the late end of this range in spring and at the early end of this range in late summer and fall.

Some species are seen in certain areas only when they are passing through. Usually, this is in spring, late summer, or fall. A winter hummingbird in the East (extremely rare except along the immediate Gulf Coast) is hardly ever the Ruby-throated Hummingbird, even though it may be common in spring, summer, and fall. The strongest possibility is Rufous Hummingbird, but several other species are possible.

You can see what birds nest as well as migrate through your state by looking at the table in Appendix A. Canadian provinces are in Appendix B. Local Audubon societies and bird clubs can provide you with more precise information about status and distribution in your area.

Please note that rarities are indeed rare, and they should not normally be expected. Hummingbirds out of their normal range should be identified with extreme caution, and then verified by experts from a local bird club or Audubon Society.

4. Field Characteristics

The fourth consideration, field marks and behavior, should be arrived at quickly. Considerations one, two, and three are preliminary homework. If a hummingbird is flitting through your flower garden, you need to get a good look at it while you can. The bird might not stay very long, and it's possible that it will never come back.

We recommend a good pair of binoculars—and at least one field guide. If you aren't accustomed to using binoculars, it may take some practice. Always remember this: If you are looking at the bird with your naked eye, all you have to do is to hold your head in that exact place, put the binoculars in front of your eyes, and then focus the binoculars.

Don't forget that you may have limited time with the bird, but you can study your field guide for as long as you wish. If possible, it would be a good idea to take notes or make a sketch of the bird.

In addition to this book, consider the following guides, which have excellent sections about hummingbirds.

- *National Geographic Field Guide to the Birds of North America,* edited by Jon Dunn and Jonathon Alderfer.
- *The Sibley Guide to Birds,* by David Sibley.

If you are more than an advanced beginner (or want to be), you can study the finer points of hummingbird identification in these two books:

- *Hummingbirds of North America: The Photographic Guide,* by Steve Howell.
- *A Field Guide to Hummingbirds of North America,* by Sherri Williamson.

As you study the hummingbird in question, here are some things to look for:

The best identification strategy is to look first at the head and bill. Males usually have an iridescent gorget; females, as a general rule, do not. Don't forget that, in different light and from different angles, a hummingbird's colors, especially on the gorget, can change. In some species, males also have an iridescent boldly colored area on the forehead and crown, which is called a helmet. When looking at the face, you should also look for the presence of a dark ear patch and horizontal lines—white, gray, or black—that extend above, below, or behind the eye.

With regard to the bill, some species like the Magnificent Hummingbird have quite long bills, while others, like the Calliope, have short bills. In a few species the bill is bright red.

It is a good idea to look next at the tail. Is it green, black, or blue? Does it have white corners? If so, how extensive is the white? Is there a rust-colored patch at the base of the tail? One should look also at the general shape of the tail: Does it seem large? Is it notched or rounded? Is it squared off at the end? When the bird is perched at a feeder, does the tail stick out beyond the end of the wing tips, come just to the wing tips, or not quite reach the wing tips?

Though it is never definitive, behavior can be a useful clue. Observe whether the tail is held relatively steady while the bird is hovering at a feeder or if the tail flaps up and down in a pumping motion.

Size is also a consideration, but it is more difficult to judge than most people realize. The farther away the bird is, the smaller it seems to be—and distance is difficult to estimate. On the other hand, if two hummingbirds are side by side at a feeder and one is noticeably larger than the other, they are most likely different species.

Hummingbird species are not all the same size

Most adult male hummingbirds can be readily identified using descriptions in this and other hummingbird books. Good pictures of all American hummingbird species are also available on the Internet. Just search on www.google.com or some other search engines, using phrases like "Anna's Hummingbird." The Google task bar is easy to install and allows you to click on an icon that searches only for pictures.

There are just a few male hummingbirds that are difficult to identify in the field: Adult male Allen's Hummingbirds closely resemble adult male Rufous Hummingbirds, the major difference being that the Allen's is green on the upper back while the male Rufous is almost always solidly copper colored on the back.

The adult males of Buff-bellied Hummingbirds of southeastern Texas and the Berylline Hummingbird of extreme south Arizona and New Mexico are also similar. Because there are no known instances of their ranges overlapping, these birds can safely be identified by where they are seen.

The males of the Ruby-throated Hummingbirds of the east and the Broad-tailed Hummingbirds of the west are superficially similar. The Broad-tailed, however, has a tail that is longer, wider, and not forked. The gorget of the Broad-tailed is more rose colored than red and the green on its back has a slight bluish cast. Also, the male Broad-tail makes a distinct whirring sound when flying; male Ruby-throats do not make this flight sound. The two can easily be separated by a consideration of where the hummingbird is seen. If you are in the Rocky Mountains, it is undoubtedly a Broad-tailed. If you are in Indiana, it can safely be called a Ruby-throat.

Identification of female and immature hummingbirds can be considerably more difficult.

5. Some Hummingbirds Are Simply Impossible to Identify

Occasionally a hummingbird will appear that even the experts can't, with any confidence, identify as to species. It is quite proper to say sometimes that you just don't know for sure. It's also quite proper to say, "Probably." In Arizona we sometimes get Allen's Hummingbirds around midsummer. Since the females and immatures are inseparable in the field from the much more common Rufous Hummingbird, we tend to say that the females and immatures are probably Rufous Hummingbirds. Some birders use the name of the genus these birds share and simply call them Selasphorus hummingbirds. If we see a full adult male that is either a Rufous or an Allen's—and if it has a full gorget plus a rufous body with a solid green back—we Arizona birders often say that it is probably an Allen's. In rare cases we are wrong, but it is a reasonable guess. We have an Allen's Hummingbird on the list of species we have had in our yard, but we are not absolutely certain. There is no universal rule about indefinite birds. Some people want absolute certainty; others are content with an identification based on high probability. It is wise to have some idea about what the odds actually are in any given area at any given time of the year.

If you aren't an advanced birder, you will end up labeling many female and immature hummingbirds as a probable or just an unknown. That's OK. The world won't end if you don't identify every single bird you see. Just enjoy them.

ENJOYING HUMMINGBIRDS

Feeding Hummingbirds

Hummingbird Gardens

Hummingbird Activities

Hummingbird Vacations

CHAPTER FIVE

FEEDING HUMMINGBIRDS

The old saying "eat like a bird" makes no sense at all! During the daylight hours a hummingbird eats almost constantly, usually at least once every ten minutes. Because eating is the primary activity of hummingbirds, it is easy to observe them in the routine of their daily lives.

The most natural and enjoyable way to watch hummingbirds is feeding on flowers. These tiny jewels stab their beaks into the blossoms of nectar-producing flowers and lap up the heavenly elixir with their long, retractable tongues. Nevertheless, the most successful hummingbird gardens contain both nectar-producing plants and artificial feeders that dispense sugar-water. This chapter will focus on the feeders.

Selecting and Using Commercial Feeders

We strongly recommend that you purchase at least one nectar feeder for your garden, patio, or window. Nectar feeders can attract hummingbirds even if you live on the second or third story of an apartment building. But don't forget the flowers. Your chances of enticing hummers quickly will be enhanced if you place the feeder near nectar-rich annuals and perennials that hummers find attractive.

Deciding Which Feeder to Buy

There are many types of commercial hummingbird feeders, and new ones are constantly appearing on the market. Opinions vary as to the best type, and the feeders that are most pleasing to look at may not necessarily be the ones most favored by the hummingbirds. You may want to try different types and then decide which works best for you and your hummingbirds. Here are some factors to take into consideration:

- Is the feeder easy to clean? How easily does it snap apart? Do I need a brush to clean it?
- Does it leak?
- Are the feeding ports spaced so that several hummingbirds can feed at one time?
- Are the feeding ports small enough to discourage or prevent bees?
- Can I see hummingbirds when they feed on ports that are on the opposite side of my viewing point?
- Does the feeder have a built-in moat to keep ants out? If not, should I buy a moat to hang just above the feeder?
- Is the feeder easy to hang? Can it be mounted on a post or attached to a window?
- Is the feeder attractive to look at? (Unfortunately, some of the most beautiful hummingbird feeders are not very functional.)
- Is the feeder too heavy?
- Is the feeder well constructed and durable?

Some Recommendations

We have fed hummers for more than 25 years and we would like to share some of our favorite feeders. All are durable and the hummingbirds approve.

First of all, we would suggest plastic hanging feeders with built-in ant moats. Here are some of the best:

- **Aspect Hummingbird Excel:** This is a 16-ounce capacity feeder with six feeding ports. It can be suspended from a built-in hanger or post mounted. The feeding ports are difficult for bees to use, and there is a built-in ant moat.
- **Aspects Hummingbird Mini:** This eight-ounce feeder is a smaller version of the Excel. It is a great choice for those territorial hummers that don't like to share or for when there are only a few hummers frequenting your garden.
- **Droll Yankee Happy Eight:** This is a 32-ounce feeder with eight ports that are widely spaced. The Happy Eight is a good choice at the peak of migration or any time there are lots of hummers around.

Another good choice would be plastic window feeders. Here's a good one:

- **Droll Yankee Window Hummingbird Feeder:** This six-ounce capacity feeder has two feeding ports. It allows us to watch hummingbirds one or two feet from our face. The ports are positioned for unobstructed viewing, and the feeder stays in place with two suction cups that are provided. Though it is not bee-proof, it is our favorite window feeder, and we've tried them all!

Some people prefer glass bottle feeders with a plastic base. These three popular feeders are a little heavy and they require a bottle brush for cleaning as well as a funnel for filling, but they rank high in attractiveness to hummingbirds. All lack flowerlike targets, but the hummingbirds have no difficulty using them.

- **Nature's Best:** This feeder comes with either an 8- or 32-ounce capacity bottle. Each has an eight-port base, and the tiny ports are bee-resistant.
- **Best-1:** This feeder has a 32-ounce capacity bottle and eight feeding ports. It has small, bee-resistant ports like the Nature's Best feeders.
- **Opus Garden Jewel:** This 10-ounce, pear-shaped feeder is glass above and has plastic bee-resistant feeding ports beneath.

Another popular type of feeder has a clear plastic nectar-filled cylinder above a red plastic base with ports that resemble yellow flowers. Here are some examples:

- **Perky Pet 211:** Holds eight ounces of nectar.
- **Perky Pet 220 Grand Master:** Holds 48 ounces.
- **Bird Company Fliteline Feeder:** This 30-ounce feeder is similar to the Perky Pet models, but has an hourglass shape.

All the feeders we have mentioned are easy to clean and durable. And the hummingbirds approve.

Some popular hummingbird feeders

Once you have selected which type of feeder or feeders to use, you might consider the following accessories:

- **HummBrella**
  This clear plastic dome is made by Aspects. It blocks the rain so the nectar will not become diluted. The solar gray color of the dome reduces evaporation, and a built-in ant guard stops crawling insects from reaching the feeder.

- **Ant Guard**
  This is a plastic cup that fits between a hummingbird feeder and the hook that holds it. Fill the cup with water and the ants will be unable to get down to the feeder.

- **HummerPlus Brush**
  Droll Yankee makes a wonderful tool for cleaning hummingbird feeders. It has a curved design that cleans the interior curves of a hummingbird feeder, and the natural bristles won't scratch your feeders.

Nectar

Even more important than the type of feeder you've chosen is what's in it. No matter how lovely a feeder may be to the human eye, for the hummer it is what's in it that counts most.

Recipe for Hummingbird Nectar
- 1 part sugar
- 4 parts water

Boil water, stir in sugar, and then boil for one to two minutes more. COOL. Fill feeders. Store remaining nectar in refrigerator for no more than one week.

Clarification: If you use one cup of sugar, use four cups of water. If you use two cups of sugar, use eight cups of water. Research has shown that this ratio most closely approximates the sugar concentration found in many hummingbird flowers.

We do not recommend commercial hummingbird nectar mixes in spite of their popularity due to the preservatives and dyes they contain. We strongly recommend that you make your own.

HUMMINGBIRD FEEDER TIPS

Hummingbirds also need protein in their diets. Placing some over-ripe fruit in your garden will attract insects and delight your hummers. Bananas work great.

NEVER offer honey to your hummingbirds. It can cause a fungus on a bird's tongue that can be fatal.

NEVER use artificial sweeteners in your hummingbird nectar. They have no food value and will not provide the birds with the calories they need.

DO NOT USE RED FOOD COLORING: Almost all hummingbird feeders have more than enough red trim to attract hummingbirds, so we see no need for adding red coloration to nectar, especially since research studies have found red dye to be harmful to small mammals. We have found no evidence that hummingbirds prefer nectar with red dye, and we know of other hummingbird enthusiasts who, in side-by-side tests, have reported that hummingbirds actually prefer the clear nectar. Another problem with red dye is that it masks the cloudiness that occurs in feeders when the nectar is going bad.

Maintaining Your Feeders

Hummingbird feeders should be cleaned thoroughly every two to three days. In very hot weather, we clean ours daily. The nectar solution is very susceptible to mold and harmful bacteria. If left in a feeder for several days, it becomes subject to fermentation. Why risk the health of these wonderful little creatures when a good scrubbing will eliminate any concerns?

> **TIP**
>
> If you have a problem with mildew, mold, or fermentation, you can use a solution of 12 parts water to 1 part chlorine bleach. Let your feeder soak for 30 minutes, then rinse thoroughly. Air-dry before filling.

Putting Out Your Feeders

Feeders should be put out at least one week, preferably two, before hummingbirds are expected to arrive in your area. It's so disheartening to spot that first migrant poking around the nail or hook where you hung a feeder last season only to be disappointed because there's no sweet treat there. And how disappointing to see it dart over to your neighbor's feeder next door.

Most hummingbird species arrive in the United States in the warmer months, though in some regions hummingbirds are found all year. Where we live in southeastern Arizona, we keep our feeders out year-round. Observing a Blue-throated, Magnificent, or Violet-crowned Hummingbird in the snow is a real thrill! You can check the migration information in our species accounts for when to expect hummers to arrive and depart in your area.

Callioipe Hummingbird

Taking Down Your Feeders

At the Hummingbird Web Site we often receive questions regarding when to take down feeders. The callers consistently have the misconception that a hummingbird will not migrate if you leave your feeder out in the fall and winter. This is a widespread myth.

Hummingbirds migrate due to instinct and not on the basis of the availability of food. Most experts believe migration is triggered by the changing length of days. If a hummingbird arrives at your feeder after migration has passed, it is probably sick, injured, or a young bird that has lost its way. Your feeder may be its sole source of survival at least until it has built enough energy to continue its journey. So don't take that feeder down too soon! You can also check the migration information in our species accounts to determine approximately when to expect hummers to depart from your area. Several years ago many species of western and Mexican hummingbirds began to show up along the Gulf Coast in winter. It was so exciting that most folks there now leave their feeders up all winter. In general, these birds leave healthy and happy in the spring.

Feeder Visitors

Hummingbird feeders may attract other creatures—some welcome, some not. At our own feeders we have had orioles, butterflies, moths, verdins, painted redstarts, acorn woodpeckers, a coatimundi, and a bear. One summer a gray fox came to our hummingbird feeders with such regularity that we were afraid he might develop diabetes.

Acorn Woodpecker at a hummingbird feeder

Bees and Wasps

"Help! My hummers can't feed for all the bees on my feeders." This is one of the most frequent complaints we receive. Our first suggestion is to be very careful in choosing your feeders. The ports of some feeders are just perfect for bees and wasps to enter. Other feeders are designed to make it a little more difficult, but none are perfect. The simplest solution was recommended to us several years ago by our dear friend and hummingbird lover Sally Spofford, who used to say: "Apply Avon's Skin-So-Soft Bath Oil. Just apply a small amount around the ports but not the hole. Also, be careful not to spill the solution on any perches so that it won't get on the hummers' feet." This was wonderful advice that really works.

Even "bee-proof" feeders can attract dozens of bees if the slightest amount of nectar splashes on the outside of the feeder. So try to avoid spills when filling feeders. If any nectar should get spilled, wipe it off with a damp cloth before it dries. And never put pesticides or harsh chemicals on your feeders.

Ants

Ants can climb up a tree trunk or a post that holds a feeder, walk out on an arm or horizontal branch, and then march down the chain or wire to invade a feeder. They can form a line with two-way traffic all the way from the ground to the hummingbird feeder. To prevent this, you can purchase a hummingbird feeder with a built-in ant moat. Fill the moat with water and ants won't be able to cross to a place where they can walk farther down. There are also ant moats—plastic cups with a hanger above and below— that can be bought as a separate attachment for any feeder that hangs. These are available in most wild bird stores and by mail order.

CHAPTER SIX

HUMMINGBIRD GARDENS

Planting for Hummingbirds

Plant flowers, flowers, and more flowers. Hummingbirds have an ongoing love affair with them. Because hummingbirds depend on nectar produced by flowering plants along with insects they glean, there has always been an intimate relationship between hummingbirds and flowers. This relationship is not one-sided, as many flowers are dependent upon hummingbirds for pollination.

Though most hummingbirds readily adapt to the commercial feeders described in Chapter Five, a small number never do. It's quite disappointing to spot a hungry hummer poking around your red-trimmed feeder but never learning to use the ports. All hummingbirds, however, are genetically programmed to feed from flowers.

Most flowers don't bloom year-round, but many of the hummers' favorites are annuals. Where possible, try to stagger the bloom time of your plantings so that there are always some plants blooming during the time hummers are in your area. Feeders provide a good backup when flowers are scarce.

Hummingbird enthusiasts and experts agree that the color red is like a magnet to hummers, followed by bright pink and orange. Some research has shown that yellow is the next color of choice. However, we have found that quite a few purple, lavender, and blue nectar-producing plants are irresistible to these tiny birds— particularly some of the *salvia*s. Hummingbirds are not genetically programmed to favor the color red, but have learned that red flowers more often than not offer a sweet treat. A hummer's favorite color is dependent on the color of the available flower that produces the most nectar.

Honeysuckle

Pink Jasmine

Getting Started

When choosing which hummingbird plants to buy, try to find someone who has a good knowledge of plants at your local nursery or garden center. Below, we will recommend some of the plants hummers prefer in different areas of the United States. Ask for these plants by their botanical names whenever possible. Often the common names are not consistent from one nursery to another and you may not take home the plant you thought you were buying.

An attractive hummingbird garden

Southwest

Because of its close proximity to Mexico, the southwest attracts more different species of hummingbirds than any other area of the country. Black-chinned, Blue-throated, Magnificent, Broad-tailed, Broad-billed, Violet-crowned, Anna's, Rufous, Costa's, and Calliope are all frequent visitors. A few other species are rare here and show up only occasionally to the delight of birders. Some species pass through during migration; others nest here and give us the opportunity to watch them care for their young. And a few individuals brighten our winters by staying all year long.

Here are some of our personal favorite hummingbird plants which, more importantly, delight the hummers that grace our gardens here in the southwest.

Parry's Penstemon

GOOD PLANTS FOR THE SOUTHWEST

SCIENTIFIC NAME	COMMON NAME
Salvia coccinea	scarlet, Texas, and tropical sage
Salvia guaranitica	anise sage, giant blue sage
Salvia leucantha	Mexican bush sage
Salvia greggii	Rocky Mountain and autumn sage
Salvia elegans	pineapple sage
Salvia splendens	red salvia
Agastache mexicana	hyssop
Chilopsis linearis	desert willow
Hamelia patens	firebush
Heuchera sanguinea	coral bells
Justicia californica	chuparosa
Lobelia cardinalis, L.laxiflora	cardinal flower
Cuphea ignea	Mexican cigar
Digitalis spp.	foxglove (needs shade)
Mimulus cardinalis, M. spp.	monkey flower
Stachys coccinea	Texas betony, scarlet hedge nettle, red mint
Penstemon parryi	Parry's penstemon
Penstemon spectabilis	showy penstemon
Penstemon pseudospectabilis	desert beardtongue
Phaseolus coccineus	scarlet runner bean
Tecomaria capensis	Cape honeysuckle
Campis radicans	trumpet vine, trumpet creeper
Lonicera japonica	Hall's honeysuckle, Japanese honeysuckle
Lonicera sempervirens	coral and trumpet honeysuckle
Ipomoea quamoclit	cypress vine
Monardadidyma, M. citriodora	bee balm
Aquilegia desertorum	Arizona columbine
Cirsium arizonicum	Arizona thistle
Zauschneria garrettii	'Mountain Flame' Mountain Flame hummingbird trumpet
Agave chryantha, A. deserti, A. parryi, A. Americana, a. scabra	Century plant

Southeast

For many years we lived in Mississippi just 70 miles north of the Gulf Coast. We were fortunate as educators to have the summers off and spent eleven summers in the Chiricahua Mountains photographing and videotaping birds. We found that some of the same plants that grow well in the southwest were also favorites of the hummingbirds in the southeast. We observed many a Ruby-throated Hummer gouging its beak into the blossoms of these and other plants, lapping up the sweet elixir. In winter, especially along the Gulf Coast, we were often fortunate enough to see several other species feeding on some of these plants.

Turks' Cap

GOOD PLANTS FOR THE SOUTHEAST

Scientific Name	Common Name
Salvia coccinea	scarlet, Texas, and tropical sage
Salvia guaranitica	anise sage, giant blue sage
Salvia leucantha	Mexican bush sage
Salvia greggii	Rocky Mountain sage, autumn sage
Salvia elegans	pineapple sage
Salvia splendens	red salvia
Abutilon hybridum, A. pictum	flowering maple
Buddleia alternifolia	butterfly bush
Lobelia cardinalis, L. laxiflora	cardinal flower
Malvavicus arboreus var, drummondii	turk's cap, sultan's turban
Nicotiana glauca	tree tobacco
Pentas lanceolata	pentas, Egyptian star
Callistemon viminalis	weeping bottlebrush
Cuphea ignea, C. micropetala, C. 'David'	Mexican cigar
Hamelia patens	firebush
Campsis radicans	trumpet vine, trumpet creeper
Impomoea coccinea	red morning glory
Impomoea quamoclit	cypress vine
Albizia julibrissin	mimosa tree
Justicia brandegeana	shrimp plant
Justicia spicigera	Orange jacobinia, Mexican honeysuckle, hummingbird bush, orange justica
Phygelius capensis	Cape fuchsia
Lantana camara, L. horrida, L. montevidensis	lantana
Lonicera japonica	Japanese honeysuckle
Lonicera sempervirens	coral and trumpet honeysuckle
Tecomaria capensis	Cape honeysuckle
Impatiens capensis	jewelweed

Western Mountains

The western mountains have many hummingbirds. This region begins in the slopes of northern Mexico and continues up through the high meadows of the Canadian Rockies. Hummingbirds love foraging on the many wildflowers along their migration path, but also can be enticed to visit your feeders and flower gardens during the spring, summer, and early fall.

Conversing with hummingbird enthusiasts and gardeners in this area was sometimes difficult. There were so many hummingbirds hovering around the blossoms in their gardens that it was difficult to keep our eyes off the birds and our minds on the plants. Nevertheless, we were able to come up with the following recommendations:

Salvia greggii

GOOD PLANTS FOR THE WESTERN MOUNTAINS

Scientific Name	Common Name
Campsis radicans	trumpet vine, trumpet creeper
Buddleia alternifolia.	butterfly bush, summer lilac
Zauschneria spp.	California fuchsia
Agastache cana	double-bubble mint
Agastache berberi	giant hummingbird mint
Monarda spp.	bee balm
Salvia coccinea	Texas sage
Salvia elegans	pineapple sage
Salvia greggii	Rocky Mountain sage
Impatiens wallerana	impatiens
Stachys ciccubea	scarlet betony
Ipomopsis aggregata	scarlet gilia
Kniphofia uvaria	red-hot-poker
Lonicera sempervirens	trumpet honeysuckle
Lilium spp.	red lilies
Delphinium sp.	prairie delphinium
Delphinum grandiflorum	butterfly larkspur
Penstemon cardinalis	cardinal penstemon
Penstemon strictus	Rocky Mountain penstemon
Penstemonvirens	blue-mist penstemon
Silene laciniata	Mexican campion

The Northeast and Canada

Each spring, Ruby-throated Hummingbirds make their way across the Gulf of Mexico. Some leave their wintering grounds from as far south as Costa Rica. Many of these hummers will choose to remain in the southeastern states to breed, nest, and rear their young. Others will stop off in the northeastern states. Some will make their way to locations as far north as Nova Scotia and Alberta. We're often asked how these tiny birds make such a long and precarious trip across the Gulf. The answer is: one tiny wing beat at a time.

Foxglove

If the weather is too cold when the hummingbirds arrive in your area, plant flowers in hanging baskets and pots that can be brought inside at night along with your feeders.

For those who want to attract a large concentration of Ruby-throated Hummingbirds to your garden, these plants will get you started.

GOOD PLANTS FOR THE NORTHEAST AND CANADA

Scientific Name	Common Name
Aquilegia canadensis	red columbine
Monarda didyma, M. citriodora	bee balm, bergamot
Monarda fistulosa	horsemint, wild bergamot
Syringa vulgaris	lilac
Lonicera sempervirens	coral honeysuckle
Phaseolus coccineus	scarlet runner bean
Elaeagnus umbellate	autumn olive
Heuchera sanguinea	coral bells
Salvia splendens	scarlet sage
Chaenomeles speciosa, C. japonica	flowering quince
Caragana arborescens	Siberian pea tree
Buddleia alternifolia	butterfly bush
Campsis radicans	trumpet creeper
Lonicera japonica	Japanese honeysuckle
Lobelia cardinalis	cardinal flower
Digitalis spp.	foxglove
Alcea rosea	hollyhocks
Impatiens capensis	jewelweed
Rhododendron spp.	rhododendrons
Kniphofia uvaria	red-hot-poker
Phygelius capensis	Cape fuchsia

The Pacific Northwest

Several species of hummingbirds visit the Pacific Northwest, but the feisty little Rufous lights up hummingbird gardens in huge numbers. Each spring these tiny balls of light fly up from Mexico to breed and nest as far north as the Yukon and Alaska

Anna's is another conspicuous hummingbird in this region. This species remains in some areas of the Pacific Northwest during the winter and is for all practical purposes nonmigratory. If you live within the winter range of the Anna's, keep your feeders out year-round and plant flowers that bloom in winter. Allen's Hummingbirds also nest in some areas of this region. You can entice them to nest in your yard by planting azalea bushes.

Below are some of the plants that will help attract several species of hummingbirds to your yard if you live in the Pacific Northwest:

Iris

GOOD PLANTS FOR THE PACIFIC NORTHWEST

Scientific Name	Common Name
Monarda sp.	bee balm
Campsis radicans	trumpet vine
Justicia brandegeana	shrimp plant
Callistemon citrinus	lemon bottlebrush
Kniphofia uvaria	red-hot-poker
Phygelius capensis	Cape fuchsia
Zauschneria californica, Z. cana	California fuchsia
Fuchsia magellanica	fuchsia
Ribes speciosum	red flowering currant
Lobelia cardinalis	cardinal flower
Salvia elegans	pineapple sage
Salvia guaranitica	anise sage, giant blue sage
Salvia splendens	scarlet sage
Digitalis spp.	foxglove
Rubus spectabilis	salmonberry
Camellia sasanqua	winter-blooming camellia
Delphinium cardinale	scarlet larkspur
Delphinium nudicaule, D. nelsonii	larkspur
Ipomopsis aggregate	scarlet gilia
Robinia pseudoacacia	black locust tree
Rhododendron spp.	rhododendron, azalea
Embothrium coccineum	Chilean flame tree
Arbutus menziesii	madrone tree
Telopea oreades	Australian flame tree
Arbutus unedo	strawberry tree
Vestia lycioides	vestia
Erica sp.	South African heather
Buddleia alternifolia	butterfly bush
Canna sp.	canna
Alcea rosea	hollyhock
Hamamelis virginiana	witch hazel

Syringa vulgaris	lilac
Mirabilis jalapa	four-o'clock
Impatiens wallerana	impatiens
Aquilegia spp.	columbine
Hibiscus syriacus	althea, rose of Sharon
Aesculus pavia var. pavia	red buckeye
Arctostaphylos spp.	manzanita
Ribes sanguineum	gooseberry, crimson-flowered currant
Iris spp.	iris
Penstemon barbatus	scarlet bugler
Penstemon cardinalis	scarlet penstemon
Penstemon eatonii	Eaton's penstemon, firecracker penstemon
Penstemon strictus	Rocky Mountain penstemon
Lonicera japonica	Hall's honeysuckle, Japanese honeysuckle

Impatiens

California

During spring and fall migrations, hundreds of thousands of hummingbirds show up in California. Several species including Rufous, Allen's, Costa's, Black-chinned, Broad-tailed, and Calliope may be seen. Anna's Hummingbird is present in some areas throughout the year. Gardening with some of the plants listed below will surely reward you with some of these delightful visitors.

Coral Fountain or Firecracker Plant

GOOD PLANTS FOR CALIFORNIA

Scientific Name	Common Name
Kniphofia uvaria	red-hot-poker
Callistemon spp.	bottlebrush
Justicia californica	Chuparosa
Justicia brandegeana	shrimp plant
Salvia elegans	pineapple sage
Salvia leucantha	Mexican bush sage
Salvia clevelandii	Cleveland sage
Salvia guaranitica	anise sage
Fuchsia lycioides	fuchsia
Fuchsia magellanica	fuchsia
Ceanothus arboreus	California lilac
Tecomaria capensis	cape honeysuckle
Lonicera involucrata	twinberry honeysuckle
Mimulus spp.	monkey flower
Albizia julibrissin	mimosa tree
Echium	Pride of Madeira (shrub)
Grevillea spp.	G. 'Robyn Gordon' (shrub)
Penstemon spectabilis	showy penstemon
Fouquieria splendens	ocotillo
Arctostaphylos spp.	manzanita
Hyptis emoryi	desert lavender
Lonicera interrupta	chaparral honeysuckle
Hibicus syriacus	althaea, rose of Sharon
Cuphea ignea, C. micropetala	David verity, Mexican cigar
Anigozanthos sp.	kangaroo paw
Ipomoea multifida	cardinal climber
Trichostema lanatum	woolly blue-curls
Lavatera assurgentiflora	tree mallow
Buddleia alternifolia	butterfly bush
Abutilon hybridum, A. pictum	flowering maple
Pentas lanceolata	pentas

The Midwest

We were pleasantly surprised at how many wonderful hummingbird plants thrive in the Midwest. One woman who lives in Wisconsin has a garden that would rival any we've seen anywhere in the United States. Following are some of the tried-and-true recommendations we've gathered from a number of gardeners in this area. Keep in mind that a number of these are annuals in this region and won't make it through the harsh winters. However, they will thrive in the warmer months and make it well worth your while in attracting hummingbirds as well as making a strikingly beautiful garden.

Salvia Coccinia

GOOD PLANTS FOR THE MIDWEST

SCIENTIFIC NAME	COMMON NAME
Salvia coccinea	Texas sage
Salvia guaranitica	anise sage, giant blue sage
Salvia Greggii	autumn sage, Rocky Mountain sage
Salvia elegans	pineapple sage
Salvia x Raspberry Delight	raspberry delight hybrid bush sage
Lobelia cardinalis	cardinal flower
Abutilon hybridum, A. pictum	flowering maple
Monarda didyma, M. citriodora	bee balm
Monarda fistulosa	horsemint, wild bergamot
Digitalis spp.	foxglove
Agastache x Desert Sunrise	hybrid hummingbird mint
Perovskia atriplicifolian	Russian sage
Phaseolus coccineus	scarlet runner bean
Buddleia alternifolia	butterfly bush, summer lilac
Heuchera sanguinea	'Firefly' coral bells
Cuphea llavea	bat-faced cuphea
Lupinus perennis	lupine
Liatris spp.	blazing star, gay feather
Lilium superbum	Turk's cap lily
Silene regia Sims	royal catchfly
Triphylla fuchsia	fuchsia 'Gartenmeister Bonstedt'

The above lists consist of plants that have proven successful over many years in attracting hummingbirds to our own gardens as well as those of hummingbird gardeners from each region of the country. We hope these recommendations will be helpful in your own gardening for hummingbirds. Space does not allow us to list every plant for each region. So don't be afraid to try some new ones on your own. We had no idea that some of our Mississippi favorites would do so well in Arizona. Some of them didn't, but many of them did.

For a more comprehensive list of hummingbird plants for each region, see "A Master Guide to Hummingbird Plants" in *Hummingbird Gardens* by Barbara Nielsen and Nancy L. Newfield. We will be forever indebted to Nancy for getting us started in gardening for hummers, and to both Barbara and Nancy for providing this valuable resource.

CHAPTER SEVEN

HUMMINGBIRD ACTIVITIES

Getting Up Close

If you stand perfectly still near a feeder, it is often possible to watch hummingbirds hovering while dipping their long tongues into nectar only two feet away from your face. Occasionally one of these miniature birds will perch right before your eyes, jerking its head from side to side. This causes the gorget to explosively lighten up, and then suddenly darken. At times like this, you can hear the buzzing of their wings and feel a rush of air. Though this experience is a little frightening to some people, the chance of being hurt by their long bills is minuscule. Terrie has been known to laugh with glee at the tickling sensation of having a hovering hummingbird peck at her red hair.

We have, without disturbing our hummingbirds, slowly moved a hand toward a feeder, and, on rare occasions, we have even touched the tip of a hummingbird's tail. We have placed an index finger below a feeder perch, eased the finger up, and then gently nudged a hummingbird's tiny feet until the bird wrapped its tiny claws around it, using our human finger as a new perch.

Other people have invented harmless hummingbird tricks. We know of a woman who held a small, shallow saucer in her palm, looking like St. Frances as hummingbirds swarmed around to feed from her outstretched hand. The most outlandish trick was when Wade Sherbrook, then director of the Museum of Natural History's Southwest Research Station in southeastern Arizona, put a dab of red lipstick on the center of his lips, balanced a small pool of sugar-water on his tongue, and actually enticed wild hummingbirds to drink out of his mouth.

The Thrill of the Chase

Many bird-watchers keep lists of all the birds they have seen. Why not make a list just for hummingbirds? The best place to start is in your own backyard. In Eastern states, there may only be one species possible, but it would still be interesting to keep a log of high numbers, sex, maturity, arrival dates, and departure dates. The next step up might be keeping a list of all the hummingbirds seen in your state. Though it is difficult to get above a total of one in New Hampshire, a huge list can be amassed in Louisiana, Mississippi, or Alabama if one lives near or can visit the coastal regions in winter. Even bigger lists are possible in Texas, Arizona, California, and New Mexico.

At the next level you would keep a list of all the hummingbirds you have seen in the United States. This would necessitate at least one hummingbird vacation in southeastern Arizona. What next? How about hummingbirds of the world? You could go to Mexico, Central America, Jamaica, Ecuador, Peru, Venezuela, Brazil, and other New World countries. We know people who have done this. We also know of people who have photographed or videotaped dozens of hummingbird species. This, of course, entails a considerable amount of travel. In the next chapter we will describe our own hummingbird trip to Costa Rica.

Collecting Hummingbird-related Items

There are several indoor, armchair activities that are related to hummingbirds. For example, you could collect hummingbird books. A search on sites like www.amazon.com can produce many possibilities. Also, there are some more difficult-to-find books that are no longer in print. A prime example is John Gould's *Hummingbirds,* a beautiful collection of hummingbird plates done more than a hundred years ago. The most recent reprint was in 1990. Anyone lucky enough to find a copy at a used book dealer should expect to pay well over $100 for it.

Many people enjoy wildlife art, and there are excellent pictures available, either as original art or as reproductions. The Gould lithographs are oversized, beautiful, and expensive. Smaller reproductions are more moderately priced. Many other art prints and reproductions by a variety of artists are easily available. The collecting of hummingbird art can be a satisfying hobby if you have enough wall space to display them.

Another popular hobby is collecting porcelain hummingbird sculptures. These range from inexpensive knickknacks to fine art worth considerable sums of money. We own several of the beautiful hummingbird sculptures made by Maruri USA. They are realistic, moderately priced, and make nice conversation pieces.

Sharing Your Hummingbird Experiences with Others

If you love hummingbirds, you are not alone. There are tens of thousands of Americans who share your interest. If you want to interact with them, there are several ways. You can join a local Audubon Society or bird club; search for Internet sites about hummingbirds and possibly join a chat group about hummingbirds and hummingbird gardening; or join one of the hummingbird organizations mentioned below. One of the best ways to mix with other hummingbird enthusiasts is to visit popular hummingbird viewing sites in southeastern Arizona or southern New Mexico in late summer. Another is to visit one of the hummingbird festivals or vacation spots described in the next chapter.

Hummingbirds as Pets

Sorry, this is not a good idea. It's also illegal. Hummingbirds, like all other American songbirds, are protected by law. You should also be aware that private hummingbird aviaries are illegal in the United States, but there are a few people in Europe who maintain them at great expense.

Surfing the Web for Hummingbird Sites

Dozens of Web sites are devoted to hummingbirds. The quality has a wide range, but almost all are fun to browse. Here are a few of our favorites.

Hummingbird World
www.hummingbirdworld.com
> This Web site was constructed by the authors, and it can be considered a supplement to this book.

Hummingbirds.net
www.hummingbirds.net
> At this excellent site, maintained by Lanny Chambers of Fenton, Missouri, you can find much information about the hummingbirds of the United States and Canada. Also, in spring, you can track the northward migration of Ruby-throated Hummingbirds.

Hummer/Bird Study Group
www.hummingbirdsplus.org
> This nonprofit organization founded by Bob and Martha Sargent of Clay, Alabama, is dedicated to the study and preservation of hummingbirds and other neotropical migrants.

Hummingbird Search Engine
www.whatbird.com
> This site by Mitchell Waite has a search engine that provides in-depth information about individual species of hummingbirds. In the SEARCH box, you can type in the name of a hummingbird species, such as "Ruby-throated Hummingbird." Or you can just type in the word "hummingbird."

Southeast Arizona Bird Observatory
www.sabo.org/hummers.htm
> This site has much information about hummingbirds and other avian species in Arizona.

The Hummingbird Society
www.hummingbirdsociety.org
> This site is a good source of information about hummingbirds and hummingbird conservation.

Wikipedia

en.wikipedia.org/wiki/Hummingbird

This multiple-author, unsigned work-in-progress provides excellent up-to-date information about hummingbirds, and it includes a useful link to a list of all the hummingbirds of the world.

More Links

For more links to hummingbird Web sites, see the links page on the Hummingbird Web site:

www.hummingbirdworld.com/h/resource.htm

Alternatively, you can use a popular search engine such as **www.google.com,** searching on the word "hummingbird" or any word or group of words that is more specific.

Making Hummingbird Houses

In general, this is not a good idea, because hummingbirds do not nest in cavities and show no interest in boxes with an entrance hole. Some western hummingbirds will choose to nest on ledges or human structures, and occasionally someone will have success building a small platform for them.

Photographing Hummingbirds

If your hummingbirds tolerate you standing close to a feeder (as they often do), you may occasionally be able to get satisfying pictures with a standard camera and a standard, relatively short lens. The problem is that the hummingbirds are so small and that they move about so quickly.

You may decide to move up to a telephoto lens so you can get more magnification. With the advent of digital photography, magnification has become easier and less expensive. Recently, we have been getting excellent results with a Panasonic Lumix camera that is lightweight and has 12-power magnification built in. If you really get serious about hummingbird photography, you may start using flash equipment with a strobe to freeze motion. Some serious hummingbird photographers use up to four flashes, including one that shines from behind to help make the bird look more three-dimensional.

It's always nice to photograph hummingbirds when they are feeding from flowers, but it is much easier to take their picture while they are using a nectar feeder. Some photographers hide a nectar feeder behind a flower so it looks like the hummingbird is feeding from the flower, even though it is drinking sugar-water. Another trick is to spray a fine mist of sugar-water on a flower, making it more likely that hummingbirds will pick the one where the camera (usually on a tripod) is focused. Some photographers put a piece of blue or green or painted poster board behind the flower or feeder where their camera is focused. This produces a less cluttered background.

As with all bird photography, it is wise to take many pictures and plan to throw away all but the best. Birds turn their heads, flick their wings, and suddenly fly off. You will find as you photograph hummingbirds that it is a good way to study their behavior, their vocalizations, and their plumage. This hobby requires patience,

Female Black-chinned Hummingbird

experimentation, a mastery of your owner's manual, and an artist's eye for good composition.

It's also pleasurable to videotape hummingbirds. We have gotten excellent results on bright overcast days, and we managed to sell more than a thousand copies of a hummingbird video made with amateur equipment.

Drawing or Painting Hummingbirds

Hummingbirds are fun to draw and paint, either from life or from photographs. Some artists strive for biological accuracy, while others use their creative imagination to capture the soul or spirit of hummingbirds in an emotionally compelling and semi-realistic way. It may be possible to do both in the same image. If this is your thing, we recommend you learn basic skills, and then develop your own style, even if your personal style may emerge after first trying to copy the styles and techniques of others. You can study what others have done at art shows, in galleries, and on the Internet.

HUMMINGBIRD ORGANIZATIONS

The Hummingbird Society

This nonprofit corporation was organized in 1996 for the purpose of encouraging international understanding and conservation of hummingbirds. They are involved in the publication and dissemination of information about hummingbirds. They promote and support scientific study as well as protect hummingbird habitat.

P.O. Box 519, Sedona, Arizona 86324
Phone: (800) 529-3699
www.hummingbirdsociety.org

Hummer/Bird Study Group

This nonprofit organization for the study and preservation of hummingbirds was founded by hummingbird banders Bob and Martha Sargent. They have active banding programs and do studies of winter vagrant hummingbirds in the eastern United States.

    P.O. Box 250
    Clay, Alabama 35048-0250
    Phone: (205) 681-2888
    E-mail: HummerBSG@aol.com
    www.hummingbirdsplus.org

The Ontario Hummingbird Project

This is an organization for hummingbird enthusiasts in Canada.

    c/o Cindy Cartwright
    4379 Bruce Road 3, RR3
    Saugeen Shores, NOH 2C7
    E-mail: hummingbirds@bmts.com
    www.ontariohummingbirds.ca

Operation Ruby-Throat

A cross-disciplinary international project, it was founded by Bill Hilton Jr. Students, teachers, and others collaborate to study the behavior and distribution of Ruby-throated Hummingbirds.

    Hilton Pond Center for Piedmont Natural History
    York, South Carolina 29745
    Phone: (803) 684-5852
    education@hiltonpond.org
    www.rubythroat.org

Humnet

This Internet resource is a Listserv (group e-mail) for people seriously interested in hummingbirds and hummingbird gardening in the southeastern United States. It is sponsored by the Museum of Natural Science, Louisiana State University.

    www.museum.lsu.edu/~Remsen/HUMNETintro.html
    To see recent posts, go to this URL: **birdingonthe.net/ mailinglists/HUMN.html**

Finding a Spiritual Connection with Hummingbirds

Most religions or spiritual practices offer opportunities and suggestions for growth in nature. The medieval Christian mystic Meister Eckhart said, "Every single creature is full of God and is a book about God." We know someone who used shamanistic drumming to take a trip to the underworld in order to find his spirit animal and find the reason he was put on this Earth. In a vision he saw a giant hummingbird that told him his mission was to honor flowers.

The hummingbird as a totem animal

Protecting Hummingbirds and Hummingbird Habitat

It's natural and wise to protect what you love. Though none of North America's hummingbirds are on the endangered species list, habitat is shrinking, and all birds, including hummingbirds, are threatened by air and water pollution, including pesticides and other chemicals. All of nature is interrelated and intertwined. Anything that helps or preserves the whole ecosystem helps to preserve and protect hummingbirds.

There are many excellent environmental groups around the country, including the Audubon Society, the World Wildlife Fund, the Sierra Club, Defenders of Wildlife, Earthjustice, and many more. All are eager to enlist volunteers and are in constant need of financial help.

Becoming an Amateur Ornithologist
(or a Professional)

If you are really serious about hummingbirds, there are a number of things you can do that will make you an amateur ornithologist. First of all, you can study hummingbirds in your neighborhood, taking notes, recording arrival and departure dates and high numbers, drawing sketches, studying nests. Some people keep a daily log of hummingbirds they have seen. We do and we have found it interesting to compare what we see on any given day with what we saw exactly one or two years before. With patience you can observe hummingbirds engaging in flight displays and other interesting behavior. Write down what you see; include the time of day, the weather, and the exact behavior witnessed. It is entirely possible that your observations may someday be published in a local Audubon Society newsletter, the newspaper, a state or regional ornithology journal, or even some national birding magazine. By watching closely you may observe behavior no one else has ever noticed.

The best way to find a nest is to watch which way a female flies after leaving a feeder. If you do find a nest and watch it, make sure to stay at a distance where the mother hummingbird will tolerate you. If there is even a hint that she is inhibited from tending the nest because of your presence, you should leave.

It may be possible for you to measure frequency of feeding, peak feeding hours, how long displays last, days of incubation, the length of the fledgling periods, etc. Professional ornithologists always try to find something they can measure or count. Follow their lead.

If you want to become a professional ornithologist yourself, you would first have to earn a college degree in biology, and then attend a graduate school where there is an ornithologist with a good reputation to be your mentor. Careers are possible in research, wildlife management, park supervision, etc. You will have to make good grades, and eventually you will have to become skilled at the use of statistics.

Watching Hummingbird Banding

Around the country there are several licensed hummingbird banders. If one is in your area, the bander may have times when interested people can watch. This may not be to everyone's taste, because the birds are caught in a trap (a box with a feeder) and then held in the hand while they are examined, measured, and banded.

Banders study population and migration trends. They weigh birds and see how much fat they have on their bodies. They sometimes verify rarities. The tiny metal bands are lightweight and are gently fitted on the hummingbirds' legs. Each has a unique number. If the hummingbird is caught by another bander or found dead, information will be gained about its migration patterns and possibly its life span.

If this interests you, you could possibly someday become an assistant or even a bander. Licenses require special training; for more information, visit the Bird Banding Laboratory Web site at www.pwrc.usgs.gov/bbl.

Hummingbird Parties

If you live in a major flyway, you could throw a hummingbird party, inviting your friends over for tea or breakfast and some hummingbird viewing. It's a pleasant and exciting way to spend a morning. One of our favorite ways to entertain is "Birds and Breakfast," which usually features waffles, fresh fruit, and swarms of hummingbirds.

Helping Injured Hummingbirds

Window Casualties

Hummingbirds sometimes fly into windows, because they misperceive that they can fly through the reflected trees and shrubbery. They also can crash into windows when attempting to approach a plant on the inside. Occasionally a hummingbird will die as a result of the ensuing collision, while others may be stunned or injured. Stunned hummingbirds may land on the ground below the window, where they will sit for a while before flying off. They may or may not be injured; and, during this vulnerable time, it is easy for a cat, hawk, or some other predator to catch them. It is wise to gently pick them up and put them in a safe place while watching to see whether they will be able to fly off with no further assistance. While watching a stunned bird, one can look for indicators of injury—gasping or bleeding are probably bad signs. Birds that do not fly off in 20 minutes need to be fed. Use sugar-water in an eye dropper. Clean up any that spills on the bird or its surroundings. Birds with serious injuries need to be referred to a trained wildlife rehabilitator with federal and state permits.

We keep a shoebox handy as a "bird hospital." It's not just for hummingbirds, but for any bird that might hit the window. The box is lined with tissue paper and it has holes poked in the lid. Though window casualties are rare, we are always prepared for them.

Hummingbirds in the House

Occasionally a hummingbird will fly in through the open door or window of a house. More commonly one will fly into a garage. This can be an exasperating experience, because the birds typically fly as high as they can, staying in the rafters or on the ledge of the highest window they can find. We know people who have found many creative solutions to this problem—like putting a feeder at an open window, or lifting a feeder up on a long pole, then gradually lowering it. One good solution is to gently but repeatedly force the hummingbird to fly, using a broom or anything with a long handle. Do this until the hummingbird becomes exhausted. After the bird becomes weary, it will be easy to catch. Gently scoop it up, making a cage with your two hands. The exhausted bird needs to be fed. Feed it sugar-water with an eye dropper, and then release it.

Helping a Young Bird that Has Fallen out of a Nest

A hummingbird nest is tiny and it usually has two young birds in it. Eventually, as they grow, they run out of room and perch on the edge of the nest where they sometimes practice flapping their wings. Occasionally they lift off too soon and then find themselves helplessly splayed out on the ground. If you find a nestling on the ground that is too immature to fly off, try to find the nest it came from. It's probably nearby. Gently pick up the bird and put it back in the nest. Stand back, making yourself as inconspicuous as possible, and watch for the mother hummingbird's return. She will not abandon the baby just because you have touched it.

Rescued baby hummingbird

Sick Hummingbirds and Hummingbirds Caught by Cats

Sick hummingbirds may sit for unusually long times on the perches of feeders while puffing out their feathers. They are likely to have their eyes closed, and their tongues may hang out of their mouth. The only hope is to contact a wildlife rehabilitator.

If your cat walks in your house with a hummingbird in its mouth, you can be assured that the hummingbird is in serious trouble. Bites often cause serious infections. Gently remove the bird from the cat's mouth and put it in a shoebox hospital, then contact a wildlife rehabilitator. The bird should be fed every 30 minutes.

The proper care of sick and injured birds is often beyond the capabilities of amateurs, no matter how good their intentions are. Your local humane society, bird club, college, zoo, or veterinarian may be able to help you find a licensed wildlife rehabilitator for advice or for transfer of the bird. If you aren't able to find anyone with the necessary skills and training, you could contact Project Wildlife in San Diego, California. Their Web address is www .projectwildlife.org/find-hummingbirds.htm; their phone number is (619) 225-9202.

CHAPTER EIGHT

HUMMINGBIRD VACATIONS

Arizona

Why would anyone want to go to Arizona in the warm months?
One reason is the unique hummingbirds that spend the summer in
the mountains in the southeastern corner of the state. Hot weather
is not as much of a problem as most people think. In mid-to late
summer, when hummingbirds are at their peak, monsoon rains
tend to cool things off. Also, the mountain sites with the best
hummingbirds tend to be about 10 degrees cooler than Tucson
and 15 degrees cooler than Phoenix. The weather can be quite
pleasant for several hours in the early morning as well as in the
late afternoon and evening. Afternoons are often hot, but rain can
have a strong cooling effect. Hummingbird enthusiasts are usually
traveling from one set of public feeders to another. They often can

Beautiful southeastern Arizona scenery

find a place to sit in the shade, but it is always a good idea to have a hat and a bottle of drinking water.

No hummingbird vacation in Arizona is complete without a visit to Madera Canyon in the Santa Rita Mountains; the town of Patagonia; Miller, Ash, and Ramsey Canyon in the Huachuca Mountains; the San Pedro riparian area; and the village of Portal on the east side of the Chiricahua Mountains. Public viewing at feeders is available in all these areas, sometimes for a nominal fee, sometimes for free. Another good stop is the Desert Museum near Tucson.

If you are traveling on your own, be sure to buy a bird-finding guide—either Rick Taylor's book *A Birder's Guide to Southeastern Arizona* or *Finding Birds in Southeast Arizona,* which is published by the Tucson Audubon Society. Both books will give you specific information about exactly where to go and what to expect. In addition, they make useful suggestions about what to bring and where to stay. During your visit you will need a field guide to the birds and probably a guide to just hummingbirds. Steve Howell's *Hummingbirds of North America: the Photographic Guide* is excellent. Sheri Williamson's *A Field Guide to Hummingbirds of North America* is also quite useful.

If you are visiting southeastern Arizona to see hummingbirds, we would strongly recommend taking some time to see some of the other unique birds found in this northern extension of the Sierra Madres. It may be your only chance to see some of the most beautiful birds in the United States—Elegant Trogons, Painted Redstarts, and many others.

If you want to hire a guide or if you are interested in a tour package that includes everything—even lodging and airport transportation—we suggest searching on the Internet. Many of these guides and tour leaders are friends of ours; they tend to be competent and pleasant.

Places to Visit in Southeastern Arizona

Bisbee

The Southeastern Arizona Bird Observatory (SABO) has hummingbird feeders and banding activities.

> Contact: Sheri Williamson or Tom Wood
> Phone: (520) 432-1388
> P.O. Box 5521, Bisbee, Arizona 85603-5521
> E-mail: news@sabo.org
> **www.sabo.org**

Green Valley

Fifteen species of hummingbirds have been recorded in nearby Madera Canyon.

> Campground: Contact United States Forest Service
> Phone: (520) 281-2296
> Rooms and cabins are available at Santa Rita Lodge, which is in the canyon. Call (520) 625-8746.

Patagonia

At the Paton Residence, at least 13 species of hummingbirds are possible between April and October. This is an excellent place to look for the Violet-crowned Hummingbird.

> Phone: (520) 394-2340

Sierra Vista

Ash Canyon Bed and Breakfast, near the Mexican border, is one of the best places to try for some of the more difficult-to-find species like Plain-capped Starthroat, Lucifer, Berylline, and White-eared. This is a bed-and-breakfast, but day visitors are welcome for a modest fee.

> Phone: (520) 378-0773
> **www.AshCanyonBandB.com**

Beatty's Miller Canyon Apiary and Orchard Co.

Located near the Mexican border, this bed-and-breakfast has cabins, hummingbird viewing areas, camping, an orchard, and trails. From spring to early fall, thousands of hummingbirds can be seen here. In recent years it has been the best place to see a large number of species.

    Phone: (520) 378-2728

    http://users.wildblue.net/beattysguestranch

Ramsey Canyon Preserve

Located south of Sierra Vista, this popular spot has recorded 14 species of hummingbirds.

    Phone: (520) 378-2785

    A bed-and-breakfast is next door. Phone: (520) 378-3010

San Pedro Riparian National Conservation Area

This preserve at the San Pedro House, east of Sierra Vista, has recorded 13 species of hummingbirds. Hummingbird banding sometimes is done on site. There are nice hiking trails along the San Pedro River.

    Phone: (520) 459-2555

Portal

Fourteen species of hummingbirds have been seen here at the scenic entrance to Cave Creek Canyon.

Cave Creek Ranch offers cabins, feeders, and beautiful grounds.

    Phone: (520) 558-2334.

The George Walker House is a pleasant bed-and-breakfast with good hummingbird feeders.

    Phone: (520) 558-2287

Portal Peak Lodge is a motel with hummingbird feeders.

    Phone: (520) 558-2223

The Southwest Research Station, has feeders open to the public from spring through fall.

    Phone: (520) 558-2396

For local information, call the Forest Service Visitor's Center at (520) 558-2221 or local guide David Jasper at (520) 558-2307.

Tucson

Arizona Sonora Desert Museum
A unique walk-through aviary allows close looks at most of the hummingbirds of Arizona. Wild hummingbirds can also be seen feeding on flowers in the nearby gardens with native flowers.

Phone: (520) 883-1380
www.desertmuseum.org

Festival of Hummingbirds

This annual event, sponsored by the Hummingbird Society, usually takes place in May in Tucson. It includes guest speakers, presentations, art shows, and botanical garden tours.

The Hummingbird Society, 249 East Main Street, Suite 9, P.O. Box 394, Newark, Delaware 19715
Phone: (800) 529-3699
www.festivalofhummingbirds.org

Other United States Hummingbird Destinations

During migration, there are certain hot spots where large numbers of hummingbirds tend to gather. Often this will entail mostly or entirely a single species—such as the Ruby-throated or the Broad-tailed. Though some of these locations don't have anywhere near the variety of species found in southeastern Arizona, the total number of individual hummingbirds can be considerably high. Late summer is often the best time for this. Following are some recommendations.

ALABAMA

Fort Morgan

Hummingbird banding by Hummer/Bird Study Group
Phone: (205) 681-2888 (Bob and Martha Sargent in Clay, Alabama)
www.hummingbirdsplus.org

CALIFORNIA

Santa Cruz

Arboretum at University of California, Santa Cruz
Allen's and Anna's Hummingbirds breed here. Other species
can be seen when they are migrating through. There is a
hummingbird trail, and a special Hummingbird Day is usually
scheduled sometime in mid-March.
> Phone: (831) 427-2998

Palm Springs

Living Desert Wildlife and Botanical Park
The botanical gardens represent various desert ecosystems and
include a hummer garden. Anna's and Costa's hummingbirds
breed here.
> Phone: (760) 346-5694

San Diego

San Diego Wild Animal Park, Escondido
In the Hidden Jungle Aviary you can see several South
American species of hummingbirds.
> Phone: (760) 747-8702
> **www.sandiegozoo.org**

San Diego Zoo, Balboa Park

The hummingbird aviary has several South American species.
Anna's Hummingbirds are common on the grounds.
> Phone: (619) 231-1515, ext. 4570
> **www.sandiegozoo.org**

Irvine

At the Tucker Wildlife Sanctuary in Modjeska Canyon, you
can see local breeders as well as spring and fall migrants.
> Phone: (714) 649-2760

LOUISIANA

Folsom

Folsom Hummingbird Festival
Mizell's Farms, 83215 Highway 25
Call or e-mail for the date of the annual festival, which
offers programs about hummingbird gardens as well as
demonstrations of hummingbird banding.
> Phone: (985) 796-9309
> E-mail: mizellfarms@yahoo.com

St. Francisville

Feliciana Hummingbird Celebration
Call or e-mail for the date of this annual event with vendors,
banding demonstrations, and programs about hummingbird
gardening.
> Phone: (800) 488-6502
> E-mail: fns@audubonbirdfest.com
> **www.audubonbirdfest.com**

NEW MEXICO

Grants

El Malpais National Monument
Huge numbers of Broad-tailed Hummingbirds can be seen here
in May as they feed on blooming Claret Cup and Paintbrush.
> Phone: (505) 783-4774 (Bureau of Land Management)

Silver City

Grey Feathers Lodge, near Lake Roberts, has recorded 11
species of hummingbird. Thousands can sometimes be seen in
August. A licensed hummingbird bander often works here.
> Phone: (505) 536-3206
> E-mail: greyfeathers@hotmail.com

Albuquerque

Rio Grande Nature Center has an annual Hummerfest
with informative talks and a chance to see hundreds of

hummingbirds. Call for date of events.
Phone: (505) 344-7240

Santa Fe

Santa Fe Greenhouses (High Country Gardens) offers an annual hummingbird and butterfly festival. Visitors can see demonstration gardens with regional native plants as well as hundreds of hummingbirds.
Phone: (800) 925-9387
www.highcountrygardens.com

Jemez Springs

In late summer or early fall migration, River Dancer Inn has been known to have thousands of hummingbirds, mostly Broad-tails.
Phone: (505) 829-3262

SOUTH CAROLINA

Operation Rubythroat

Operation Rubythroat has ongoing projects in the United States, Canada, and Costa Rica.
www.rubythroat.org
Contact: Bill Hilton Jr.
E-mail: hilton@rubythroat.org

TEXAS

Big Bend National Park

This remote but beautiful national park has many interesting hummingbirds, including Lucifer and Blue-throated.
Phone: (915) 477-2251

Fort Davis

Davis Mountain State Park, in a remote area of west Texas, has recorded 15 species of hummingbird. Camping is permitted.
Local contact: Kelly Bryan
Phone: (915) 426-3337 or (915) 426-3533

The Prude Guest Ranch near Fort Davis maintains numerous hummingbird feeders. Sometimes hundreds of hummingbirds can be seen here. The ranch has cabins and an RV park.
Phone: (915) 426-3201

Bayside
The Fennessey Ranch offers hummingbird tours, which include attention to native flowers that are attractive to hummingbirds. In addition to the many hummingbirds (sometimes thousands), more than 400 species of birds have been seen on the property.
Phone: (512) 529-6600
E-mail: fennessey1@aol.com

Rockport/Fulton
The Hummer/Bird Celebration has been an annual event in this area since 1989. It has been known to attract as many as 5,000 hummer lovers plus thousands of hummingbirds. Numerous hummingbird experts offer programs and tours to local homes with hummingbird gardens. There are even birding trips by boat and bus. Contact the Rockport-Fulton Chamber of Commerce for the dates of the event and further information.
Phone: (800) 826-6441

The Kennedy Residence in Rockport has many feeders that attract up to 2,000 hummingbirds in September. In addition to the numerous Ruby-throats, they get Buff-bellied hummingbirds and four other species. They offer a bed-and-breakfast for birders.
Phone: (512) 729-7009

San Antonio
The Rio Frio Guesthouse at Rio Frio in the nearby Hill Country offers nesting Black-chinned Hummingbirds, plus Rufous and Ruby-throated Hummingbirds when they are

migrating. Hundreds—perhaps more than a thousand—hummingbirds can be seen at the peak of migration.

Phone: (210) 735-1696

San Angelo

The Texas Gems Hummer House in nearby Christoval, has thousands of Black-chinned Hummingbirds from April through August. Other species can be seen in migration, and sometimes on-site banding takes place at this bed-and-breakfast. Please call ahead.

Phone: (915) 255-2254

South of the Border

As much as we enjoy North American hummingbirds, they represent only a small fraction of all the hummingbirds in the world. While 19 species of hummingbird have occurred in the Unites States and 6 in Canada (some of these being extreme rarities), an amazing variety of other hummingbirds is found in Mexico, the Caribbean, Central America, and South America. There are more than 300 hummingbird species worldwide—all in the western hemisphere—and 95 percent of these species are found only south of the border between the United States and Mexico.

A HUMMINGBIRD VACATION IN COSTA RICA

Curious about hummingbirds in other parts of the Americas, we booked a trip to Costa Rica. After flying into San Jose, we spent the night at Hotel Bougainvillea. While waiting for our driver the next morning, we strolled through the hotel's extensive gardens where we were happily entertained by several Rufous-tailed Hummingbirds that were cavorting among the lush, nectar-rich flowers. We also saw our only Steely-vented Hummingbird of the trip, as well as other remarkable Costa Rican birds like the oversize and exotic-looking Blue-crowned Motmot, which has a huge racquet-shaped tail.

Rancho Naturalista, our primary destination, was a 2.5-hour drive from San Jose. We spent a week at this lovely and comfortable lodge, eating beautifully prepared meals and gazing at a splendid variety of hummingbirds. Whenever we looked at the feeders on our second-floor balcony we saw swarms of White-necked Jacobins, Rufous-tailed Hummingbirds, Green-breasted Mangoes, Green-crowned Brilliants, and Violet-crowned Woodnymphs. Each day on our private balcony as well as on the public balcony, we had the opportunity to see Brown Violet-ears, Green Hermits, and Violet Saber-wings as they darted from feeder to feeder. Some of the shier hummingbird species were usually seen only in the first hour or so of daylight. Green Thorntails, Stripe-throated Hermits, Violet-headed Hummingbirds, and Black-crested Coquettes were all excellent reasons to rise early.

"Rancho Naturalista" in Costa Rica

A memorable hummingbird destination

White-necked Jacobin

Gray-tailed Mountain Gem

Snowcap

Violet-crowned Woodnymph

Brown Violet-ear

Green-crowned Brilliant

After a festive breakfast on the patio spent talking to other guests and enjoying the tanagers and collared aricaris as they ate bananas and other fruit from nearby bird feeders, we often took a short hike to the woodland hummingbird feeders where we saw more Jacobins, Violet-crowned Woodnymphs, Green Hermits, and Violet Saber-wings. At this forest station we saw other interesting species, like the Red-footed Plumeleteer and a tiny hummingbird that can, for all practical purposes, be seen nowhere else: the Snowcap. We also had the good fortune of observing a hummingbird not normally seen at Rancho, the Band-tailed Barbthroat.

Rancho Naturalista has a special treat for Hummingbird lovers. Late in the afternoon, we took a short hike on another trail that twists through the dark woods and ends at a 20-foot-deep gorge where water trickles through, forming numerous shallow pools. There in the waning light of the day, we looked down in amazement as various species of hummingbirds came to bathe. The hummingbirds would appear out of nowhere, hover over the water, then plunge briefly just deep enough to wet their bellies and splash water over their backs. In the brief moment they were in the water they would lean forward to wet their throats. Then they would rise a couple of feet above the water to dive again—and sometimes yet again. Though daylight was waning, the colors of the hummingbirds were often brilliant, perhaps because of reflected light on the water below them. At this magical spot we saw Jacobins, Plumeleteers, and Woodnymphs, but the star of the show was the hummingbird our guide said was his favorite—the Purple-crowned Fairy. This bird is rarely seen during earlier parts of the day, because of its habit of feeding high in the trees. The fairy, dark above and pure white below, is longer and thinner than most other hummingbirds and has an unusually short bill. Its glory is in the long white tail feathers, which flash outward like expanded fingers while the bird is hovering over a dark pool, preparing to dive. Our guide, Herman, said the fairy looks like a miniature woodpecker when it uses its short but strong bill to glean insects from the bark of tall trees. It even makes a tapping sound.

From our guides we learned much about Costa Rican hummingbirds. They introduced us, for example, to a type of hummingbird with which we have had no previous experience: the hermits. There are about 34 species in this tropical subfamily. Their plumage is usually some combination of green, brown, rufous, and grey. Hermits have long, decurved bills and two elongated, white-tipped feathers extending from the center, lower end of their tail. Male hermits usually congregate in groups where they sing and make displays to attract visiting females who enter the lek as shoppers, picking out the gentleman who puts on the best show. As it approaches one of the feeders at Rancho Naturalista, the Green Hermit almost forms a semicircular arc with its long, decurved bill, its arched back, and its unusually long tail. The longer-tailed female, with two stripes on her face, is especially striking. Occasionally we saw the much smaller and browner Stripe-throated Hermit near the main lodge feeding on the verbena bushes, often appearing out of nowhere. The Band-tailed Barbthroat is also a member of this unique family.

The hummingbird we had to work the hardest to see was the most elaborately decorated—the Black-crested Coquette. We needed to be at its favorite bush between 5:30 and 6 a.m. to watch it for ten minutes or so before the larger and more aggressive hummingbirds arrived to chase it off. This tiny hummingbird has an orange beak and a black chest. It has a white band across its rump. The male has long black streamers extending far back from the top of its head and also, but to a lesser degree, from the sides of its green gorget. The belly of this little treasure is covered with bronze spots.

The most unusual-looking hummingbird, at least to us, was the female Green-breasted Mango, who has a bold, dark streak down the center of her white throat and belly.

Everyone who goes to Rancho Naturalista wants to see the Snowcap, and few are disappointed. We saw it daily. The tiny male is mostly a deep purple color, but his white cap glows as if lit from within, even in the darkest forest. There is something brash, virile, and self-confident about this tiny bird as it chases away much larger hummingbirds. Even when he lands on a bare branch, the forward tilt of his white cap and the slight upward slant of his bill make him look as brave and cocky as Popeye.

The Violet-crowned Woodnymphs were common but somehow mysterious. Often they look entirely black; then, as they turn to catch a bit of reflected sunlight, they suddenly burst forth into deeply saturated shades of purple, green, and black. It is as if a fairy godmother touches them with a magic wand, changing their drab attire into an elegantly sequined gown. In the last chapter of this book we give our favorite literary allusion to the hummingbird, a passage from *Green Mansions,* by William Henry Hudson. The novel was based on Hudson's experiences in Central America, and we cannot help but think that this was the very hummingbird he was referring to.

We saw the Green Thorntails only in the early morning, before the more aggressive hummingbirds became active. This short-billed green hummingbird, like the coquette, has a white band across the rump. The wings and tail are black. In the male the tail is quite long and has two sharp points.

The Violet Saber-wing is large and quite dark, purple on the head and underparts, and dark green on the back, wings, and tail. As it approaches a feeder or flower, it flashes large white areas in the tail. Like the Red-footed Plumeleteer, it tends to make brief, aggressive forays toward the feeders, perching in the meantime about 20 to 30 feet away in the dark recesses of the forest.

The White-necked Jacobin has a deep blue head and a striking tail that is mostly white. True to its name, it has a white band on the back of the neck.

As intriguing as the hummingbirds are here on the Caribbean Slopes, it is virtually impossible to not pay attention to the splendid variety of other avian species. We took many hikes into the dense montane forest where we saw more than a dozen species of tanagers as well an endless variety of exotic birds, like the White-collared Manakin and the Squirrel Cuckoo. We saw Keel-billed Toucans, two species of parrot, two kinds of trogon, and many other interesting birds. On the trails we saw glass-winged and morpho butterflies. The most beautiful trees were the poros, or mountain immortalities, which, to our good fortune, were full of orange flowers. Oropendolas, Blue-gray Tanagers, and many other types of birds feasted in these magnificent trees all day long. Our excellent guides, Herman and Leo, helped us find about 130 species of birds we had never seen before at Rancho, as well as numerous neotropical migrants that we knew from their summer sojourns north to the United States, where they build nests and raise babies before returning to their ancestral home in Central America.

During our week at Rancho, we took a few side trips. We spent one full day at Irazu Volcano National Park where we added Fiery-throated Hummingbird, Volcano Hummingbird, Scintillant Hummingbird, and Green Violet-ear to our list. One morning, in the beautiful Platanillo River Valley, we saw a heronlike bird called a Sun Bittern. We had the good fortune of seeing it sun itself by stretching out huge wings that were patterned like a Navajo blanket.

After leaving Rancho Naturalista, we spent a few days at a high-elevation spot in the cloud forest of Savegre Valley, which is about three hours south of San Jose. Here we found a new species of hummingbird, the Gray-tailed Mountain Gem. Green Violet-ears and tiny Scintillant Hummingbirds were abundant, as was the Magnificent Hummingbird, the only species of hummingbird we saw in Costa Rica with which we had previous experience in the

United States. In the Savegre Valley we also saw what is the most famous and, arguably, the most beautiful bird in the world, the Resplendent Quetzal. Our guide, Marino, called it the "movie star."

The male Mountain Gem is green with a white throat and a pale blue-green crown. We thought the female more beautiful than the male; her entire underside is a rich cinnamon color.

We had been eager to spend more time with the Green Violet-ear. This hummingbird is a rare straggler to the United States, but a total stranger to our eager eyes before the brief looks we got a few days before at Irazu Volcano. We were delighted to find that the Green Violet-ear is common at the Savegre feeders. As we watched, we discovered that this sleek, mostly green hummingbird has a subtle beauty that grows with repeated viewings. The iridescent violet ears, hardly noticeable at first, actually flare out when the bird becomes excited. As we watched the Violet-ears, we developed an appreciation for the subtle ways the green plumage changes into patches of blue, and we also came to notice a dark band across the lower part of the tail. One afternoon we saw a scruffy, newly fledged Green Violet-ear (that only a mother could love) as it perched clumsily atop one of the feeders at Savegre Mountain Lodge. The young bird held its long beak wide open whenever a member of its species came to the feeder, and occasionally it got fed by the one that was its real parent. We cheered when this ratty, disoriented, fluffed-up mess of feathers discovered a port and inserted its long tongue to—for the first time perhaps—lap up nectar with no assistance.

Contact information for Costa Rica

Lodges

Rancho Naturalista (near Turrialba)
Lodge phone: 011-506-554-8100
Phone/Fax: 011-506-554-8101
E-mail: info@ranchonaturalista.net
www.ranchonaturalista.net

Savegre Mountain Lodge (near San Gerardo de Dota, south of Cartago)
P.O. Box 482 Cartago, Costa Rica
Phone: 011-506-740-1028
Fax: 011-506-740-1027
www.savegre.co.cr/indexeng.html

Travel Agencies

Costa Rica Gateway
Sbo 840 P.O. Box 025292
Miami, Florida 33102-5292
Phone: (888) 246-8513
E-mail: crgateway@racsa.co.cr
www.costaricagateway.com

Travel Excellence
1551 NW-82 Avenue, Suite 506-108
Miami, Florida 33126
Phone: (506) 258-1046
E-mail: info@travelexcellence.com
www.travelexcellence.com

These are the approximate numbers of hummingbird species that occur in some other countries south of the United States border.

Ecuador: 163
Brazil: 84
Colombia: 136
Mexico: 50
Peru: 100
Argentina: 24
Venezuela: 97

The following is a sampling of some colorful names of the hummingbirds to be found in these countries: Sunangels, Metaltails, Thornbills, Pufflegs, Brilliants, Lancebills, Sabrewings, Starfrontlets, Woodstars, Emeralds, Sapphires, Goldenthroats, Jewelfronts, Racket-tails, Helmetcrests, Trainbearers, Sylphs, Shining Sunbeams.

Exotic hummingbirds can best be found with the help of a tour guide, and there are many companies that offer this service. Here are some that we personally recommend.

Asa Wright Nature Center (In Trinidad)
Phone: (800) 426-7781 (Caligo Ventures)
www.asawright.org

Borderland Tours
Borderland also does an annual hummingbird tour in southeastern Arizona, led by hummingbird expert Rick Taylor.
2550 West Calle Padilla
Tucson, Arizona 85745
Phone: (800) 525-7753
E-mail: info@borderland-tours.com
borderlandtours.com

Eagle-Eye Tours
P.O. Box 750
Windermere, British Columbia, V0B 2L0
Canada
Phone: (800) 373-5678

E-mail: travel@eagle-eye.com
www.eagle-eye.com

Field Guides
9433 Bee Cave Road
Building 1, Suite 15
Austin, Texas 78733
Phone: (800) 728-4953
E-mail: fieldguides@fieldguides.com
www. fieldguides.com

Mark Smith Nature Tours
P.O. Box 3831
Portland, Oregon 97208-3831
Phone: (360) 566-0458
E-mail: pamd@wittravel.com
www. marksmithnaturetours.com

Victor Emanuel Nature Tours
2525 Wallingwood Drive
Suite 1003
Austin, Texas 78746
Phone: (800) 328-8368
E-mail: info@ventbird.com
www.ventbird.com

Wings
1643 North Alvernon Way, Suite 109
Tucson, Arizona 85712-3350
Phone: (888) 293-6443
E-mail: wings@wingsbirds.com
www.wingsbirds.com

To find more locations and tour companies, we recommend
searching on the Internet.

Hummingbird Legends

Hummingbirds in History, the Arts, Science,
and the Popular Imagination

CHAPTER NINE

HUMMINGBIRD LEGENDS

Native American Mythology

Because hummingbirds are found only in the Western Hemisphere, they are absent from the traditional fairy tales, legends, and myths of European-and African Americans. There is, however, a rich supply of stories about these tiny birds in Native American mythology.

A Mayan legend says the hummingbird is actually the sun in disguise, and he is trying to court a beautiful woman, who is the moon. Another Mayan legend says the first two hummingbirds were created from the small feather scraps left over from the construction of other birds. The god who made the hummers was so pleased, he had an elaborate wedding ceremony for them. First butterflies marked out a room, then flower petals fell on the ground to make a carpet. Spiders spun webs to make a bridal pathway, then the sun sent down rays that caused the tiny groom to glow with dazzling reds and greens. The wedding guests noticed that whenever he turned away from the sun, he became drab again like the original gray feathers from which he was made.

A third Mayan legend speaks of a hummingbird piercing the tongues of ancient kings. When the blood was poured on sacred scrolls and burned, divine ancestors appeared in the smoke.

A Mojave legend tells of a primordial time when people lived in an underground world of darkness. They sent a hummingbird up to look for light. High above them the little bird found a twisted path to the sunlit upper world where people now live.

There is a legend from the Jatibonicu Taino Tribal Nation of Puerto Rico about a young woman and a young man who were from rival tribes. Like Romeo and Juliet, they fell in love, precipitating the intense criticism of their family and friends. Nevertheless, the two of them found a way to escape both time and culture. One became a hummingbird and the other a red flower. The Taino Indians also take the hummingbird to be a sacred pollinator whose mission is to bring an abundance of new life.

To the Chayma people of Trinidad, hummers are dead ancestors, so there is a taboo against harming them. An extinct Caribbean tribe called the Arawacs thought it was Hummingbird who brought tobacco. They called him the Doctor Bird.

In a Navajo legend a hummer was sent up to see what is above the blue sky. It turns out to be absolutely nothing.

In a Cherokee story, a medicine man turned himself into a hummingbird to retrieve lost tobacco plants. In another Cherokee story, a woman is courted by both a hummingbird and a crane. She first chooses the hummingbird for his good looks, but the crane convinces her that there should be a race around the world with the winner having her hand in marriage. She agrees, thinking the hummingbird is bound to win because he flies so fast. What she fails to take into account is that Crane can fly all night long, while Hummingbird is able to fly only during the day. When Crane wins, she reneges on her promise, because he is so ugly. The Creek Indians have a similar story. In this version Crane wins because he flies in a straight line, while Hummingbird zigzags.

Hopi and Zuni legends tell of hummingbirds intervening on behalf of humans, convincing the gods to bring rain. Because of this, people from these tribes often paint hummingbirds on water jars. The Hopi kachina for Hummingbird depicts him with green moccasins and a green mask. He has an aqua body and is yellow on top of the head; he is crowned with a ruff made of Douglas fir.

One of the Hopi stories is about a time of famine when a young boy and girl were left alone while their parents were searching for food. After the boy made a toy hummingbird, his sister threw it into the air. It came to life and began to provide for them by bringing an ear of corn every day. Eventually, the hummingbird flew to the center of the earth where it pleaded with the god of fertility to restore the land. Rain and green vegetation came; then the children's parents returned.

In a Pima legend a hummingbird acted like Noah's dove, bringing back a flower as proof the great flood was subsiding.

There is a legend from Mexico about a Taroscan Indian woman who was taught how to weave beautiful baskets by a grateful hummingbird to whom she had given sugar-water during a drought. These baskets are now used in Day of the Dead festivals.

An Apache legend tells of Wind Dancer, a young warrior, who was born deaf but could sing magical, wordless songs that brought healing and good weather. He married Bright Rain, a beautiful young woman whom he rescued when she was being attacked by a wolf. Wind Dancer was killed during another errand of mercy. A bitter, death-bringing winter ensued, but it suddenly and mysteriously ended after Bright Rain started taking solitary walks. Tribal elders learned Wind Dancer had come back to her in the form of a hummingbird. He wore the same ceremonial costume and war paint he had worn as a man. In fields of spring flowers he would approach her and whisper his magical secrets in her ear. This brought her peace and joy.

The Pueblo have hummingbird dances and use hummingbird feathers in rituals to bring rain. Pueblo shamans use hummingbirds as couriers to send gifts to the Great Mother who lives beneath the earth.

To many of the Pueblo, the hummingbird is a tobacco bird. In one myth, Hummingbird gets smoke from Caterpillar, the guardian of the tobacco plant. Hummingbird brings smoke to the shamans so they can purify the earth.

Some Pueblo have a ritual for babies who are stillborn or die in the first few days of life. Prayer sticks with hummingbird feathers are held before the sunrise on the winter solstice in a ceremony that hastens rebirth.

One Pueblo story tells of a demon who is blinded after losing a bet with the sun. In anger he spews out hot lava. The earth catches fire. A hummingbird then saves the beautiful land of people and animals by gathering clouds from the four directions. Hummingbird uses rain from these clouds to put out the flames. This legend says the bright colors on a hummingbird's throat came after he fled through the rainbow in search of rain clouds.

In Central America the Aztecs decorated their ceremonial cloaks with hummingbird feathers. The chieftains wore hummingbird earrings. Aztec priests had staves decorated with hummingbird feathers. They used these to suck evil out of people who had been cursed by sorcerers.

An Aztec myth tells of a valiant warrior named Huitzil, who led them to a new homeland, then helped them defend it. This famous hero's full name was Huitzilopochtli, which means "hummingbird from the left." The "left" is the deep south, the location of the spirit world. The woman who gave birth to Huitzil was Coatlicul. She conceived him from a ball of feathers that fell from the sky. Huitzil wore a helmet shaped like a giant hummingbird.

In an important battle, Huitzil was killed. His body vanished and a green-backed hummingbird whirred up from the spot where he had fallen to inspire his followers to go on to victory. After Huitzil's death, he became a god.

Blue-throated Hummingbird

The Aztecs came to believe that every warrior slain in battle rose to the sky and orbited the sun for four years. Then they became hummingbirds. In the afterlife these transformed heroes fed on the flowers in the gardens of paradise, while engaging from time to time in mock battles to sharpen their skills. At night the hummingbird angels became soldiers again and followed Huitzil, fighting off the powers of the darkness, restoring warmth and light. As dawn broke, the hummingbirds went into a mad frenzy. The sun rewarded them for this by giving them a radiant sheen.

In an Aztec ritual, dancers formed a circle and sang a song which included these words: "I am the Shining One, bird, warrior, and wizard." At the end of the ritual, young men lifted young girls, helping them to fly like hummingbirds.

There is another Aztec legend that says the god of music and poetry took the form of a hummingbird and descended into the underworld to make love with a goddess, who then gave birth to the first flower.

One widespread belief is that hummingbirds, are messengers between worlds. As such, they help shamans keep nature and spirit in balance. The Cochti have a story about ancient people who lost faith in the Great Mother. In anger, she deprived them of rain for four years. The people noticed that the only creature who thrived during this drought was Hummingbird. When they studied his habits, the shamans learned that Hummingbird had a secret passageway to the underworld. Periodically, he went there to gather honey. Further study revealed that this doorway was open to Hummingbird alone because he had never lost faith in the Great Mother. This information inspired the people to regain their own faith. After that the Great Mother took care of them.

CHAPTER TEN

HUMMINGBIRDS IN HISTORY, THE ARTS, SCIENCE, AND THE POPULAR IMAGINATION

History

When European settlers first came to America they quickly learned that hummingbirds had a special significance to indigenous people. The pilgrims, for example, met Native American ambassadors who wore hummingbird earrings. European soldiers and missionaries in Mexico met Aztec kings who wore cloaks made entirely of hummingbird skins.

As white Europeans claimed ownership to the land and eventually came to be owned by the land, they began to integrate hummingbirds into their own way of seeing. These glittering elves, unknown in the Old World, seemed magical and fascinating. This new race of Americans began wondering what caused these flying gems to darken and then brilliantly light up. They must have asked: Why such gratuitous and extravagant colors? And how could they be so little? One common belief was that hummingbirds were a cross between an insect and a bird. Another was that, in autumn, hummingbirds stick their long beaks into the trunks of trees and die, only to resurrect again in the spring.

One folk belief that still persists is that hummingbirds migrate on the backs of geese or swans.

Even Christopher Columbus wrote of hummingbirds in his diary. And just a few years after his discovery of the New World, a hummingbird skin found its way to Rome as a gift to the Pope. One of America's earliest nature writers, Hector St. John de Crevecouer, wrote this of the hummingbird:

> Its bill is as long and as sharp as a coarse sewing-
> needle; like the bee, nature has taught it to find out in the

calyx of flowers and blossoms those mellifluous particles that can serve it for sufficient food; and yet it seems to leave them untouched, undeprived of anything that our eyes can possibly distinguish. Where it feeds it appears as if immovable, though continually on the wing: and sometimes, from what motives I know not, it will tear and lacerate flowers into a hundred pieces; for, strange to tell, they are the most irascible of the feathered tribe. Where do passions find room in so diminutive a body? They often fight with the fury of lions, until one of the combatants falls a sacrifice and dies. When fatigued, it has often perched within a few feet of me, and on such favourable opportunities I have surveyed it with the most minute attention. Its little eyes appear like diamonds, reflecting light on every side; most elegantly finished in all parts, it is a miniature work of our great parent, who seems to have formed it smallest, and at the same time the most beautiful, of the winged species.

By the middle of the 19th century there was a large market for hummingbird skins in Europe. Hundreds of thousands of hummingbirds were being killed in South America and shipped to markets in London and other cities, where millions of skins were being purchased for collections as well as for making artificial flowers, "dust catchers," and other ornaments. It soon became fashionable for ladies to wear hats gaudily decorated with hummingbird skins.

Art

In the 19th century, hummingbirds began to appear in art. Between 1829 and 1832, R. P. Lesson published a three-volume monograph with color plates. Between 1849 and 1861, England's John Gould published a five-volume monograph with 360 hand-colored lithographic plates of hummingbirds. Many of these pictures are quite beautiful, even though they were painted from stuffed specimens. Today Gould's lithographs are collectors' items, selling for premium prices. Gould saw his first live hummingbirds in 1857 when he traveled to America. America's most famous bird artist, John James Audubon, called hummingbirds "glittering garments of the rainbow," and he painted many of them. Like Gould, he used dead specimens as models. Contemporary artists are more likely to work from photographs of live birds or while observing birds coming to feeders.

Today hummingbirds appear on almost every imaginable kind of decorative art, from teacups to T-shirts, from jewelry to wallpaper. For both professional and amateur artists, the hummingbird is a perennial favorite, and hummingbirds are popular motifs in the contemporary decorative and fine arts of numerous Native American tribes.

Literature

Many American poets have honored hummingbirds. When Emily Dickinson saw a Ruby-throated Hummingbird in her garden, she wrote these lines:

> He never stops, but slackens
> Above the Ripest Rose—
> Partakes without alighting
> And praises as he goes,
>
> Till every spice is tasted—
> He, the best Logician,
> Refers my clumsy eye—
> To just vibrating Blossoms!
> An Exquisite Reply!

In his novel *Green Mansions,* W.H. Hudson wrote:

> Have you ever observed a humming-bird moving about in an aerial dance among the flowers—a living prismatic gem that changes its colors with every change of position—how in turning it catches the sunshine on its burnished neck and gorget plumes—green and gold and

flame-colored, the beams changing to visible flakes as they fall, dissolving into nothing, to be succeeded by others and yet others.

In its exquisite form, its changing splendor, its swift motions and intervals of aerial suspension, it is a creature of such fairy-like loveliness as to mock all description.

And have you seen this same fairy-like creature suddenly perch itself on a twig, in the shade, its misty wings and fanlike tail folded, the iridescent glory vanished, looking like some common dull-plumaged little bird sitting listless in a cage?

D. H. Lawrence once wrote a poem about the dawn of creation when an enormous hummingbird was flying out on the leading edge of time as the world took shape behind it. Real hummingbirds, of course, are tiny, but there is a sense in which the world is indeed created anew every time a hummingbird flies. When our eyes follow them, we see beauty unfolding.

Here is an inspiring quote from an essay by novelist Henry Miller:

When you are convinced that all the exits are blocked, either you take to believing in miracles or you stand still like the hummingbird. The miracle is that the honey is always there, right under your nose, only you were too busy searching elsewhere to realize it. The worst is not death but being blind, blind to the fact that everything about life is in the nature of the miraculous.

At the Hummingbird Web Site, we have received numerous e-mails over the years telling of people who, after a difficult time in their lives, awakened to joy once more after watching a hummingbird. The single-minded focus of a hummingbird teaches us all how to be present in the eternal now. Beauty is always here, but sometimes we can't see it unless we hover for a moment like a hummingbird.

Science

The first biologist to describe hummingbirds in a scientific treatise was Carolus Linnaeus, who in 1758 published accounts of 18 species in his *Systema Naturae.* An 18th-century French naturalist named Buffon also attempted to catalog and describe these interesting little creatures that he called "flybirds." In 1878 an important monograph about hummingbirds was published by D.E. Eliot. In 1890 Robert Ridgeway published another monograph about hummingbirds, which contemporary ornithologist Paul Johnsgard calls "still the most valuable and definitive single volume on hummingbirds of North and Central America, particularly for its keys and plumage descriptions."

In 1940 A.C. Bent published classic accounts of the life histories of 18 North American species of hummingbirds. In 1945 James Patterson published a classification system for hummingbirds, which has become the standard authority. And in 1973 Alexander Skutch published *The Life of the Hummingbird.* This excellent book had color illustrations by Arthur Singer.

Today the best scholarly works on the biology of North American hummingbirds are probably Paul Johnsgard's *The Hummingbirds of North America* and a numbered series called *The Birds of North America,* which is written by various authors and printed by the Smith-Edwards-Dunlap Company of Philadelphia with support from the American Ornithologists Union, Cornell Laboratory of Ornithology, and the Academy of Natural Sciences.

Popular Culture

There is a common folk belief in Mexico that hummingbirds bring love and romance. In the pre-Columbian world, stuffed hummingbirds were worn as lucky charms to bring success in matters of the heart. In Mexico, even today, dead hummingbirds are sold as amulets, and powdered hummingbirds can be bought in packets. Powdered hummingbird is also used as an added ingredient in colognes and votive candles. There is a practice, still persisting, of drying the heart of a dead hummingbird, then grinding it into a powder to be used in love potions. Perhaps you

Violet-crowned Woodnymph from Costa Rica

and someone special should get a pair of binoculars and watch what's happening in the flower garden. One never knows what interesting developments might occur. However, we certainly don't recommend grinding hummingbirds into a powder.

To many New Age people in contemporary America, hummingbirds have a special meaning as a spirit or totem animal. In tattoo parlors the hummingbird is a popular design for body art, and many commercial products have hummingbird logos.

The Joy of Hummingbirds Revisited

Nothing in nature captures the eye like hummingbirds. When they hover in a sunbeam, flashing their metallic, boldly colored gorgets, they set the imagination on fire. Tradition has associated hummingbirds with the rainbow, with jewels, and with the fairy realm. Hummers dart through woods or meadows like tiny elves who know exactly where they want to go. They whir, buzz, and zoom from one splash of color to the next, approaching red or blue flowers with wing beats so fast all can we see is a blur.

The on-again-off-again beauty of hummingbirds is ethereal. Their feathers seem to glow with inner light. When we close our eyes, the images of these lively little beings seem to linger on the backs of our eyelids. If we let them, they fly directly into the soul, bypassing all our ideas and theories.

As creatures that live and have their being in fields of irises and penstemons, hummingbirds often pause magically in the air, defying gravity, aiming their needle-like beaks into the sweet inner mysteries of the flowers they love. They plunge in headfirst, half disappearing. Coming back out, they fly backwards, sometimes covered with pollen. Hummingbirds are fully alive and insanely happy. These dazzling little creatures have radiance. They give the human heart something it deeply needs.

It has been seriously suggested that dinosaurs evolved into birds. It's hard to believe this when you look at a hummingbird feeding on the snapdragons in your garden. Did brontosaurs shrink to become this glittering jewel that flies upside down and backwards while dipping his long beak and even longer tongue into the secret nectar of flowers? Is this the plodding dinosaur that walked on thick legs and shook the earth with every step?

On the Nazca plain in southern Peru, ancient artists carved out an image of a hummingbird so large it can only be recognized at about 1,000 feet in the air. Since this massive image can't be far from the place where, in primordial times, the first hummingbird opened its eyes to the pale light of dawn, we like to think of it as a cornucopia from which all the world's hummingbirds spewed out, gleaning insects, inspecting flowers, building nests, evolving, taking on kaleidoscopic variations of color and shape, spreading their range to rain forests and to the high peaks of the Andes, and then onward to Argentina, Mexico, Louisiana, Colorado, New England, and even to Alaska. For us and for many like us, hummingbirds are a joyful obsession. We believe that, whenever we give them our undivided attention, we are honoring the spirit of the land.

STATE	REGULAR (M = Migration Only)	RARE (N = Has Nested) (? = Not Confirmed)
ALABAMA	Ruby-throated	Allen's Anna's Black-chinned Blue-throated Broad-billed Broad-tailed Buff-bellied Calliope Green Violet-ear Magnificent Rufous
ALASKA	Rufous	Anna's Calliope Costa's Ruby-throated
ARIZONA	Allen's—M Anna's Berylline Black-chinned Broad-billed Broad-tailed Calliope—M Costa's Lucifer Magnificent Rufous—M Violet-crowned White-eared	Bumblebee Cinnamon Plain-capped Starthroat Ruby-throated

STATE	REGULAR (M = Migration Only)	RARE (N = Has Nested) (? = Not Confirmed)
ARKANSAS	Ruby-throated	Allen's Anna's Black-chinned Broad-billed Broad-tailed Buff-bellied Calliope Green Violet-ear Magnificent Rufous
CALIFORNIA	Allen's Anna's Black-chinned Broad-tailed Calliope Costa's Rufous	Blue-throated Broad-billed Green Violet-ear Magnificent Ruby-throated Violet-crowned Xantus'
COLORADO	Black-chinned Broad-tailed Calliope Rufous—M	Anna's Blue-throated Broad-billed Costa's Green Violet-ear Magnificent Ruby-throated
CONNECTICUT	Ruby-throated	Rufous
DELAWARE	Ruby-throated	Allen's Broad-tailed Rufous
DISTRICT OF COLUMBIA	Ruby-throated	Black-chinned Rufous
FLORIDA	Ruby-throated	Allen's Anna's Bahama Woodstar Black-chinned Broad-billed Broad-tailed Buff-bellied Calliope Cuban Emerald Magnificent Rufous

STATE	REGULAR (M = Migration Only)	RARE (N = Has Nested) (? = Not Confirmed)
GEORGIA	Ruby-throated	Allen's Anna's Black-chinned Broad-billed Broad-tailed Calliope Magnificent Rufous
HAWAII	(NONE)	
IDAHO	Black-chinned Broad-tailed Calliope Rufous	Anna's
ILLINOIS	Ruby-throated	Allen's Broad-billed Rufous
INDIANA	Ruby-throated	Rufous
IOWA	Ruby-throated	Rufous
KANSAS		Allen's Anna's Black-chinned Broad-billed Broad-tailed Calliope Costa's Magnificent Ruby-throated–N? Rufous
KENTUCKY	Ruby-throated	Black-chinned Green Violet-ear Rufous
LOUISIANA	Ruby-throated	Allen's Anna's Black-chinned Blue-throated Broad-billed Broad-tailed Buff-bellied Calliope Green Violet-ear Magnificent Rufous

STATE	REGULAR (M = Migration Only)	RARE (N = Has Nested) (? = Not Confirmed)
MAINE	Ruby-throated	Calliope Green Violet-ear
MARYLAND	Ruby-throated	Rufous
MASSACHUSETTS	Ruby-throated	Allen's Black-chinned Calliope Rufous
MICHIGAN	Ruby-throated	Anna's Broad-billed Green Violet-ear Rufous
MINNESOTA	Ruby-throated	Anna's Calliope Costa's Green Violet-ear Magnificent Rufous
MISSISSIPPI	Ruby-throated	Allen's Anna's Black-chinned Broad-billed Broad-tailed Buff-bellied Calliope Green Violet-ear Rufous White-eared
MISSOURI	Ruby-throated	Anna's Black-chinned Calliope Green Violet-ear Rufous
MONTANA	Black-chinned Broad-tailed Calliope Ruby-throated Rufous	Anna's Costa's
NEBRASKA		Broad-tailed Ruby-throated—N? Calliope Rufous

STATE	REGULAR (M = Migration Only)	RARE (N = Has Nested) (? = Not Confirmed)
NEVADA	Anna's Black-chinned Broad-tailed Calliope Costa's Rufous	Allen's Broad-billed Magnificent
NEW HAMPSHIRE	Ruby-throated	Rufous
NEW JERSEY	Ruby-throated	Allen's Anna's Black-chinned Calliope Rufous
NEW MEXICO	Black-chinned Blue-throated Broad-billed Broad-tailed Calliope—M Lucifer Magnificent Rufous—M Violet-crowned	Allen's Anna's Berylline Cinnamon Costa's Green Violet-ear Plain-capped Starthroat Ruby-throated White-eared
NEW YORK	Ruby-throated	Anna's Calliope Rufous
NORTH CAROLINA	Ruby-throated	Allen's Anna's Black-chinned Broad-billed Broad-tailed Calliope Green-breasted Mango Green Violet-ear Rufous
NORTH DAKOTA		Ruby-throated Rufous
OHIO	Ruby-throated	Calliope Rufous
OKLAHOMA	Ruby-throated	Anna's Black-chinned Broad-billed Broad-tailed Calliope Green Violet-ear Rufous

STATE	REGULAR (M = Migration Only)	RARE (N = Has Nested) (? = Not Confirmed)
OREGON	Anna's Black-chinned Calliope Rufous	Allen's—N Broad-billed Broad-tailed Costa's
PENNSYLVANIA	Ruby-throated	Calliope Rufous
RHODE ISLAND	Ruby-throated	Rufous
SOUTH CAROLINA	Ruby-throated	Black-chinned Blue-throated Broad-billed Buff-bellied Calliope Rufous
SOUTH DAKOTA	Ruby-throated	Broad-tailed Calliope Rufous
TENNESSEE	Ruby-throated	Allen's Anna's Black-chinned Broad-tailed Calliope Rufous
TEXAS	*Eastern Texas:* Ruby-throated *Central and west Texas:* Black-chinned *Rio Grande Valley and Coast:* Buff-bellied *Far West Texas and Big Bend:* Anna's Blue-throated Broad-tailed Lucifer Magnificent Rufous—M Violet-crowned	Allen's Berylline—N Costa's Broad-billed—N? Calliope Green-breasted Mango Green Violet-ear Rufous (regular migrant in far west Texas) White-eared—N?

STATE	REGULAR (M = Migration Only)	RARE (N = Has Nested) (? = Not Confirmed)
UTAH	Black-chinned Broad-tailed Costa's Rufous—M	Anna's Broad-billed Calliope—N Magnificent Ruby-throated
VERMONT	Ruby-throated	Rufous
VIRGINIA	Ruby-throated	Allen's Black-chinned Green Violet-ear Rufous
WASHINGTON	Black-chinned Calliope Rufous	Anna's Broad-tailed Costa's
WEST VIRGINIA	Ruby-throated	Green Violet-ear Rufous
WISCONSIN	Ruby-throated	Anna's Broad-billed Green Violet-Ear Rufous
WYOMING	Black-chinned Broad-tailed Calliope Rufous	Anna's Blue-throated Broad-tailed Magnificent Ruby-throated

APPENDIX B:
CANADIAN HUMMINGBIRD INFORMATION

In Canada, Ruby-throated Hummingbirds breed from central and southern Alberta to Nova Scotia. Typically they arrive in May or early June and depart in August or early September.

Rufous Hummingbirds breed in British Columbia and southwestern Alberta, where they arrive as early as March and depart in August.

Black-chinned Hummingbirds are an uncommon breeder in the southern interior of British Columbia. They arrive in May and are gone by September.

Calliope Hummingbirds breed in interior British Columbia and southwestern Alberta. They arrive in May and depart in August.

Anna's Hummingbirds are regular but uncommon in southern British Columbia.

PROVINCE	REGULAR	RARE
ALBERTA	Ruby-throated Calliope Rufous	Anna's Black-chinned Costa's Green Violet-ear
BRITISH COLUMBIA	Anna's Black-chinned Calliope Rufous	Allen's Costa's Ruby-throated Xantus'
MANITOBA	Ruby-throated	Broad-tailed Rufous
NEW BRUNSWICK	Ruby-throated	Black-chinned Broad-billed Rufous
NEWFOUNDLAND	Ruby-throated	Rufous
NORTHWEST TERRITORIES		Ruby-throated Rufous
NOVA SCOTIA	Ruby-throated	Rufous

PROVINCE	REGULAR	RARE
ONTARIO	Ruby-throated	Broad-billed Green Violet-ear Rufous
PRINCE EDWARD ISLAND	Ruby-throated	
QUEBEC	Ruby-throated	
SASKATCHEWAN	Ruby-throated	Black-chinned Calliope Rufous
YUKON		Rufous

INDEX

Academy of Natural Sciences,
176
Activities, hummingbird-related
become an ornithologist, 137–38
begin a log of your sightings, 129
building houses/platforms, 132
collectibles and books, 129–30
drawing and painting, 134
environmental protection, 137
help with banding operations, 138
human contact with the birds,
28, 128
hummers as pets, 130
join clubs and organizations, 130,
134–36
photography, 132–34
spiritual growth through, 134–35
surfing for hummer Web sites,
130–32
Aggressivness
Albino hummingbirds, 85–86
Blue-throated Hummingbird, 4
courtship and flight displays, 22–25
fighting over food, 25
Rufous Hummingbird, 6, 76
Alabama, 131, 134–35, 146
Alaska, 2, 90
Albino and hybrid hummingbirds,
85–87
Albuquerque, N.M., 149
Alderfer, Jonathan, 92
Allen's Hummingbird (*Selasphorus
sasin*), *37*
adaptation and range, 3, 6, 90, 147
courtship and dive displays, 25
description and characteristics,
37–39
Altshuler, Coug, 19
American Ornithologists Union, 176
Anna's Hummingbird (*Calypte anna*),
40
adaptation and range, 90, 147
aggressive display, 25
courtship and dive displays, 23–24
description and characteristics,
40–42
male role in nesting, 29
song/musical calls, 26
West Coast migrations, 3
Ants, dealing with, 99, 102, 107
Argentina, 162
Arizona
adaptation and species variety, 3–6

hummingbird tours and vacations,
129, 142–46
Southeastern Arizona Bird
Observatory (SABO), 144
Arizona Sonora Desert Museum, 143,
146
Artificial sweeteners, 103
Artwork and sculptures, 129–30, 134,
173–74
Audobon, John James, 174
Audobon Society, 91, 130, 137

Bahama Woodstar (*Calliphlox
evelynae*), 82, 90
Banding programs
Hummer/Bird Study Group,
134–35, 146
Louisiana, 148
SABO, 144
San Pedro Riparian National
Conservation Area, 145
Texas Gems Hummer House, 151
as a way to become involved, 138
Band-tailed Barbthroat (*Threnetes
ruckeri*), 156–57
Bayside, Tex., 150
Beauty, recognizing, 175, 177–78
Bee Hummingbird (*Mellisuga
helenae* or *zunzún*), 13, 61
Bees and wasps, 106–07
Behavior. *See also* Aggressivness
aerodynamics of flight, 19–21
as aid to identification, 91–94
courtship and flight displays, 8,
22–25
male role in nesting, 29
mating, 12, 22
musical calls, 26
torpor and sleep, 29
Bent, A. C., 176
Berylline Hummingbird (*Amazilia
beryllina*), *43*
Arizona range, 6, 144
description and characteristics,
43–44
Big Bend National Park, 149
"Bird hospital," 139–41
Bird houses, building, 132
*A Birder's Guide to Southeastern
Arizona* (Taylor), 143
The Birds of North America,
176
Bisbee, Ariz., 144

Page number of photographs are shown in ***Bold italics***.